BENCH STRENGTH

BENCH STRENGTH

*Developing the Depth and Versatility
of Your Organization's Leadership Talent*

Robert Barner, Ph.D.

⥜AMACOM

American Management Association

New York • Atlanta • Brussels • Chicago • Mexico City • San Francisco
Shanghai • Tokyo • Toronto • Washington, D.C.

Special discounts on bulk quantities of AMACOM books are
available to corporations, professional associations, and other
organizations. For details, contact Special Sales Department,
AMACOM, a division of American Management Association,
1601 Broadway, New York, NY 10019.
Tel.: 212-903-8316.   Fax: 212-903-8083.
Web Site: www.amacombooks.org

This publication is designed to provide accurate and authoritative
information in regard to the subject matter covered. It is sold with the
understanding that the publisher is not engaged in rendering legal,
accounting, or other professional service. If legal advice or other expert
assistance is required, the services of a competent professional person
should be sought.

Library of Congress Cataloging-in-Publication Data

Barner, Robert (Robert W.)
     Bench strength : developing the depth and versatility of your
organization's leadership talent / Robert Barner.
          p.   cm.
     Includes bibliographical references and index.
     ISBN-10: 0-8144-0884-2
     ISBN-13: 978-0-8144-0884-1
     1. Leadership.   2. Executive ability.   3. Executives—Training of.
I. American Management Association.   II. Title.

HD57.7.B3665   2006
658.4'092—dc22
                                                    2005030959

Printing number

10   9   8   7   6   5   4   3   2   1

CONTENTS

PREFACE

We live in an age in which an organization's distinguishing competitive advantage is not in the unique technology that it employs, nor in the markets it controls, but in its ability to develop, and make superior use of, an exceptional leadership team.

Quite frequently I hear executives and HR professionals refer to talent management as if it were an exact science. They talk as if leadership talent decisions are made with the same cold, dispassionate logic that an accountant would apply to the analysis of a variance chart. I hear this, particularly, from those HR colleagues who speak with pride of the profusion of complicated data sheets and evaluation forms that they employ for evaluating leaders or for identifying successor candidates.

In reality, leadership talent decisions take place not within some sterile planning room that is hermetically sealed off from the rest of the organization, but rather within the messy, political, and often-chaotic backdrop of the human organization. The fact is that talent management is not a science. It is, instead, an art form that is practiced by savvy executives who know how to make leadership recruitment, assessment, development, and deployment decisions that support their overarching business strategy.

I've written this book with the assumption that you are one of these leaders, and that you've picked up this book because you are looking for ways to become a better talent strategist. If you are looking for details on how to master the detailed tactical considerations of talent management, such as how to create competency models or write succession plans, I recommend that you skip this book and instead take a look at one of my earlier books, *Executive Resource Management.*

In contrast, I wrote *Bench Strength* to help executives, trainers, and OD/HR practitioners tackle some of the toughest strategy decisions that they face in determining how to manage and deploy their leadership talent. Some of the strategic issues that you will find covered in this book include:

- What you need to look for in selecting a chief talent officer (CTO)

- What basic principles you need to consider when designing a leadership talent strategy

- How to navigate decisions involving talent focus (the *Make or Buy Decision*), talent succession (the *Pool or Stream Decision*), and talent acquisition (the *Trade-Up or Build-Out decision*)

- How to maximize organizational effectiveness through effective talent deployment

- How to use "war-game scenarios" to test the viability of your talent management strategy

- How to move quickly to correct bad talent management decisions

I believe that you'll find the style of this book to be informal and nonacademic. In writing *Bench Strength,* I've tried to picture myself sitting across from you and talking with you as if I were a consultant whom you've employed to share advice on how to wade through difficult talent management decisions. This is a role that I've taken on many times in my twenty-five years as a senior organizational consultant to CEOs and other senior-level executives.

I hope that you get a lot out of this book and that you consider it a resource worthy of adding to your business shelf. If you have any questions, or simply want to engage in dialogue on some of the topics that I've covered in this book, you can feel free to e-mail me at ibscribe@earthlink.net.

Now let's get to the heart of it.

ACKNOWLEDGMENTS

I would like to acknowledge several people and organizations that were instrumental in helping me complete this book by granting me permission to reference relevant research studies in the area of talent management. I'd like to thank Patrick Kulesa, global research director for ISR, LLC, for allowing me to share with you the excellent research that ISR has done in the area of mapping leadership competencies to organizational requirements. Special thanks also goes out to Jean Martin and Carl Rhodes, respectively managing director and practice manager for the Corporate Leadership Council, for allowing me to reference what I believe to be cutting-edge research in the area of high-potential assessment and development. As always, the folks at CLC remain at the front edge of relevant HR research.

Thanks also to Mark Karelse, vice president of people and organizational development for Philips Medical Systems, for granting me permission to reference the solid work that Royal Philips Electronics, NV is doing in customizing management assessment and development efforts at the varying levels of the leadership pipeline. Finally, I would like to acknowledge McKinsey & Company for granting me permission to reprint materials related to some very timely research on the perceived value of different leadership development activities.

BENCH STRENGTH

CHAPTER 1

TALENT STRATEGY

The Key to Organizational Effectiveness

Strategy without tactics is the slowest
route to victory. Tactics without strategy
is the noise before defeat.

—SUN TZU, CHINESE MILITARY STRATEGIST

CEOs and senior executives are quickly coming to the conclusion that a distinguishing characteristic of successful organizations is the ability to identify, develop, and deploy exceptional leadership talent. Research such as the 1997 McKinsey study, *The War for Talent*, and McKinsey's 2000 follow-up study have made business managers and HR leaders aware of the significant gaps that exist between their talent management requirements and their ability to successfully execute against these requirements.

Since then, these conclusions have been reinforced by several other research studies. More specifically, when we look at the data there are five conclusions that we can draw about the current state of leadership talent management.

1. *Many companies feel unprepared to capture and develop the leadership talent that they need to succeed.* In one survey that spanned 264 executives from six countries, almost two-thirds of

1

respondents rated the ability to develop effective leaders as critical to addressing marketplace challenges, yet only 8 percent felt confident in their ability to manage leadership talent.[1]

2. *Executives feel that during the next few years, these leadership challenges will become even greater.* Only about 25 percent of surveyed companies were confident in their ability to have in place the high-potential talent that they would need to drive future growth.[2]

3. *The projected shortfall of leadership talent is likely to affect ALL sections of our talent pipelines, not just retiring baby boomers.* By 2020, executives believe the United States will experience a 15 percent reduction in professionals within the 35 to 44 age group—the age segment that has traditionally constituted a critical part of the high-potential (HIPO) leadership pipeline.[3]

4. *Most organizations are just beginning to address these talent issues.* Only 24 percent of respondents in one online survey on leadership talent indicated that their organizations had a clear plan for developing leadership talent, and only 29 percent indicated that their organizations were effective in connecting talent management to the needs of their business units.[4] Over half of respondents surveyed in one study indicated that their leadership talent identification and development system had been in place less than three years.[5]

5. *The challenge of building a strong leadership team is a global organizational issue, extending well beyond the borders of the United States.* A recent Hewitt study cited findings from previous research studies that conclude that management turnover in Chinese companies may be as high as 40 percent, with many other Asian companies reporting that they face critical challenges in developing their leaders.[6]

The Emergence of the Chief Talent Officer

One area in which the new emphasis on talent management is reflected is in the evolving role of the Human Resources department.

In many organizations, HR leaders are being asked to outsource or de-emphasize transactional HR activities such as payroll and employee benefits, so that they can take on broader, more influential roles as talent strategists. Some organizations have gone so far as to formalize this role transition under the titles of chief talent officer (CTO), or vice president of talent management. For the more cynical among us, it's important to understand that these role shifts and title changes represent more than a semantic shell game. Instead, they reflect an evolution in the mind-set of corporate executives, as organizations come to understand the way in which talent management can drive organizational performance.

The fact is that executives are looking for HR and OD (organization development) leaders who are able to go beyond managing a set of isolated recruiting, development, and training activities, to be able to articulate a viable game plan for capturing and leveraging leadership talent. For their part, organizational leaders are being expected to play a stronger role as coauthors of this game plan. As a result of these changes, today in almost every organization, executives and HR leaders are being held more accountable for the talent decisions that they make.

It All Starts with Strategy

So if talent management is so critical to organizational success, how do you go about building a stronger leadership bench? The major point that I'll be making throughout this book is that an effective organizational approach to talent management proceeds from a well-considered and clearly articulated strategy. Unfortunately, the term "strategy" is frequently misunderstood. When I ask executives to discuss their organizations' leadership talent strategies, they often start off by discussing their 360° feedback programs, executive coaching, or assessment centers. The truth is that while such talent management tools and tactics can be very valuable, they don't come close to constituting a talent management strategy.

To explain what I mean, let's start with an agreed-upon definition of what we mean by the term "strategy." At an organizational level, a strategy can be viewed as being *a flexible game plan that enables an organization to deploy its resources in a way that ensures dominance within a competitive field of play.* As it applies to talent management, a strategy is *a flexible game plan for acquiring, strengthening, and deploying an organization's leadership talent to ensure the best long-term competitive advantage for one's organization.*

The most effective strategies, whether they are formed to guide a sports team, or an organization, share five common characteristics. A review of these characteristics serves as a useful starting point for introducing the concept of talent strategy development:

1. Strategies come into play only in the presence of a competitor.

2. Strategies are defined in terms of the key decisions we make.

3. Strategies require a thorough knowledge of the playing field.

4. Strategies are secured through the use of a flexible game plan.

5. Strategies are realized through effective deployment.

Characteristic #1: Strategies Come into Play Only in the Presence of a Competitor

This is true regardless of whether your competitor is an opposing football team, or another company that is trying to eat your lunch. After all, how much strategy is required for a game of solitaire? With regard to talent strategies, this principle suggests that you can't base good talent management decisions solely on how your managers perform against internal, historic benchmarks. An effective talent strategy gauges bench strength not only against internal standards, but also on how leaders measure up in one's industry and competitive market. To assess your understanding of this point, why don't you take a minute to jot down your answers to the following questions, then compare your answers with the ones I've provided:

A Brief Exercise: How Do You Gauge Your Talent?

1. When you evaluate the leadership potential of one of your managers, what is your basis for comparison?
2. Can you name your top three talent competitors?
3. How insular is your business unit? That is, to what extent does your department or division tend to look inward when identifying future talent or making talent decisions?

What Your Answers Tell You

Question 1: *What is your basis for evaluating a leader's performance and potential?*

Answer: While many managers base their answers solely on a comparison of other leaders within their organizations, it's possible to go beyond this measure to assess talent against the best performers in one's market. Put another way, how would your best internal candidates fare if they were forced to compete for their jobs against the best performers in their field? If you don't know, a little research is in order. Later on, in Chapter 8, I'll outline several methods for calibrating your talent against external performers.

Question 2:   *Can you name your top three talent competitors?*

Answer: By this I mean not only market competitors, but
              also those companies that would be most inter-
              ested in stealing your best people. A few years
              ago, I worked for an international logistics com-
              pany that began losing a few key people to a
              small business start-up in a noncompetitive field.
              We quickly traced the defections back to a for-
              mer executive who had left his position to help
              form the start-up company. Staying on top of this
              issue enabled us to put together an effective plan
              for retaining other likely targets for this poaching
              activity. How about you? If you were to take a
              look at the last series of voluntary terminations
              that have occurred among your high potential
              leaders, would you see a pattern of defections in
              these losses? If you don't know, investigate.

Question 3:   *How insular is your business unit?*

Answer: That is, to what extent does your department or
              division tend to look inward when identifying fu-
              ture talent or making talent decisions? In con-
              ducting leadership talent reviews across multiple
              divisions and operating companies, one of the
              things that I've discovered is that those business
              units that have the weakest talent pools tend to
              be those that foster excessive "in-breeding." In
              other words, these business units erect thick bar-
              riers between themselves and the rest of their or-
              ganization, and they attempt to keep their
              leaders tightly cloistered behind their walls. One
              of the best ways to not only accurately assess tal-
              ent, but also to build the capabilities of your lead-
              ers, is to continually place them within settings

that force them to calibrate their performance against other companies and organizational units. Task forces and mixed project teams are examples of techniques you can use to see how your leaders perform within a broader, more expansive context.

Characteristic #2: Strategies Are Defined in Terms of the Key Decisions We Make

If a strategy is one's overall game plan for obtaining and securing competitive advantage, then the essence of strategy lies in the ability to take actions that support, and align with, that strategy. There are a variety of different talent approaches that can be put into play to build leadership capability, each of which revolves around a different set of decisions. A good strategist not only makes the right decisions, but also learns to delineate, from all potential decisions that could be addressed at any one time, *those few that are critical to maintaining competitive advantage.*

A clear illustration comes from the airline industry. As I write this, most airlines are struggling to stay airborne. One of the few exceptions is Southwest Airlines, which was smart enough to hedge its bets in 2004 by locking in fuel prices long before the onset of the fuel crisis brought on by Hurricane Katrina. In this case, someone at Southwest was astute enough to look ahead and spot the build up of this change wave before it came crashing down on the industry, then take the next logical step to understand the long-term financial impact of this particular pricing and contracting decision.

In the case of talent management, one of the pivotal questions that talent strategists face is the "make or buy" decision (discussed in detail in Chapter 4), in which an organization opts to focus its bench-building efforts around either *making* leadership capacity through internal development, or *buying* extra leadership capacity through the large-scale importing of outside talent. Once set into the play, this decision becomes a very powerful force for determining how an organization frames its leadership talent strategy, and sets into motion certain critical tradeoffs in the commitment of time, resources, and executive focus. In this way, the decision to follow a given "make" or a "buy" strategy carries with it the implicit willingness to forego, delay, or minimize other competing alternative bench-building activities.

Characteristic #3: Strategies Require a Thorough Knowledge of the Playing Field

Any student of military history knows the truth of this statement. One of the most famous historical examples of this principle comes from the Battle of Agincourt. In this decisive battle in 1415, Henry V of England led his small group of foot soldiers to a dramatic defeat over a much larger French army that was largely comprised of armored cavalry. Henry won, in large part, because he took full advantage of the unique conditions presented by that battlefield. By positioning his troops in a narrow gap that lay between two thickly wooded areas, Henry forced the French cavalry's attack to be compressed into a narrow area. This action limited the full abilities of the French cavalry and exposed their horsemen to a rain of arrows from Henry's bowmen. In addition, a heavy rain had soaked the field, making it difficult for the heavily armed French knights to fight against Henry's more lightly armored and nimble soldiers. The French lost despite the use of a much stronger military force because they failed to adapt their plans to the realities of this particular battlefield.

Just as battlefield commanders attempt to exploit the advantages offered by their particular playing fields, in much the same way it's important to ensure that the leadership talent strategy that you design fully exploits the opportunities offered up by your organizational playing field. This means understanding both the external business environment and the internal organizational structure in which that strategy is enacted. It also requires that you know how to make an accurate assessment of your *leadership talent capability—the extent to which you have in place the leadership talent needed to successfully execute against your organization's goals.*

A BRIEF EXERCISE: EVALUATING YOUR PLAYING FIELD

Do you know your playing field? To find out, take a second to answer the following six questions:

1. Among the most important members of your executive team, which leaders represent your greatest retention risks? (If you don't know, you need to take a closer look at your executive team.)

2. How many times during the past two years has your organization been caught off guard by the sudden defection of high-potential talent? (Frequent, unanticipated losses can signal a lack of understanding of leaders' career goals and market-based compensation requirements.)

3. Have you ever been surprised by seemingly small talent management problems? In other words, are you quick to recognize the first warning signs of emerging talent problems? (An example would be the "stellar performer" who, upon closer review, is found to have significant derailment issues that had been readily visible to his team, customers, and peers, but which were repeatedly ignored as representing an important leadership issue.)

4. If you were put on the spot right now to identify someone to head up a new business project, do you know who you'd select as your top three candidates? How comfortable would you feel if you were called upon to defend your recommendations? (Anyone can make talent recommenda-

tions, but are they defensible? Do you know how to match leadership strengths to changing business requirements?)

5. Continuing with this last question, suppose you were given unlimited financial resources and asked to conduct a raiding party for external talent to head up this project. Could you name two organizations that would be at the top of your raiding list? (The ability to answer this question is usually an indication that you know how to calibrate your leaders' performance against the best in your industry.)

6. Pick any senior executive position in your organization. Do you have in place right now three internal candidates who could come up to the plate as qualified successor candidates for this position? Do you know what development gaps each of these candidates would have to fill in order to be considered to be fully prepared for the new position? (If you can't answer this question, you may need to obtain a more detailed and complete view of your leadership bench strength.)

Looking at your answers to these questions, how did you do? Are you comfortable with how well you know your company's business challenges and the organizational structure and talent you have available to meet these challenges, or do you need to take a closer look at your playing field? Before moving on, one other point to consider is that by asking these questions of your direct reports you can quickly determine who, within your team, has an in-depth understanding of your organizational talent.

Characteristic #4: Strategies Are Secured Through the Use of a Flexible Game Plan

A business strategy is more than a collection of financial reports and tactics for gaining market share or increasing revenue. It's an articulation of how an organization can best focus its resources and energy to achieve certain overriding, long-term goals. A company's strategic plan serves as its playbook for coordinating activity, focusing effort, and developing capabilities.

A word of caution is in order here. Keep in mind that the word "formal" doesn't have to translate into "rigid" or "lock-step." Occasionally I hear business strategy described as if it were some type of seamless plan that, once enacted, unfolds in a predictable, clockwork fashion. Sounds good, but life seldom works that way. It's more accurate to think of a business strategy as being a fluid design that can be quickly adjusted to address emerging opportunities or setbacks. As I'll discuss in detail in Chapter 9, the fact is that any strategic endeavor unfolds within a dynamic field of play. Savvy talent strategists understand this principle and are always on the lookout to exploit any talent opportunities that may arise through changing conditions.

Characteristic #5: Strategies Are Realized Through Effective Deployment

According to an old sports story, a reporter once asked the football coach Vince Lombardi whether he was ever worried that someone might steal his famous playbook. Lombardi replied that he could give his opponent his playbook and still win because winning was a matter of flawless execution.

This story, I believe, says a lot about the essence of strategy. Regardless of how thorough or detailed a job one does in strategic planning, this effort is useless without seamless execution and deployment. For the talent strategist, this means having the ability to leverage the organization's strongest leaders against its biggest business challenges. Effective deployment supports the retention of exceptional leaders and enables the organization to adapt more readily to unanticipated problems, such as the sudden departure of star players. It also requires the understanding of the subtleties of timing the execution of talent management activities.

Thinking Like a Talent Strategist

Now that we've reviewed the importance of developing a talent strategy, we need to tackle the big job of formulating and implementing a strategy. The remaining chapters are designed to guide you through the creation of a leadership talent strategy.

Chapter 2 discusses the role played by the chief talent officer (CTO) and provides guidelines for CTO selection and management. In that chapter, you'll learn why the role of the CTO has become so important to organizational success and will review several criteria you can use for CTO selection and evaluation. It also provides several suggestions for leveraging the talents of your CTO. For those readers who currently head up organizational talent management efforts, this chapter can prove useful in helping you benchmark your performance, evaluate the competencies of your direct reports, and engage your senior executives in dialogues on the roles and accountabilities of the position of chief talent officer.

In the third chapter, you will learn how to develop a clearer, more detailed view of emerging leadership talent needs by identifying both your organization's long-term goals, and the changing nature of the external business environment. Chapters 4 to 7 lay out the respective trade-offs and pay-offs associated with five critical decisions associated with the areas of talent development, recruitment, and deployment. Chapter 4 introduces six guidelines for managing difficult talent decisions, and highlights the impact of five key talent trade-off decisions that guide the talent management function, while Chapter 5 focuses on the first of these decisions, the "make or buy" decision. The next two chapters discuss when to implement alternative options for developing and acquiring talent, and review the respective pitfalls and payoffs associated with each of these choices.

In Chapters 8 through 11, you will be introduced to guidelines for talent strategy implementation. You may find it helpful to share key points from these chapters with executives and HR leaders in your company as a centerpiece for reaching alignment on a collective, organizational approach to leadership talent strategy. Chapter 8 discusses how to leverage leadership talent through creative talent deployment. Since even the best-laid plans can sometimes go off course, the final three chapters are designed to help you anticipate and resolve talent strategy implementation issues.

Chapter 9 shows you how to prepare for unexpected events that represent unforeseen threats to, or opportunities for, strengthening your leadership pipeline. This chapter also shows you how to construct "war-game scenarios" to test the robustness of proposed leadership talent initiatives against certain change scenarios, and explains how to use this scenario planning to gain executive alignment on your proposed talent strategy.

In Chapter 10, you'll discover metrics and measures for tracking your organization's overall progress on talent management objectives, and learn how the evaluation measures that you implement convey strong symbolic messages to the rest of your organization about how you define the "success" of bench-building programs. The final chapter, Chapter 11, introduces you to the seven warning signs of a bad hire and the five warning signs of a bad promotion. It also provides guidelines for conducting mid-course corrections on bad talent decisions.

Together these topics provide a coherent frame for proceeding from the broadest considerations of the design of leadership talent strategies, to the implementation, testing, and continual refinement of those strategies.

Notes

1. Hap Brakeley, Peter Cheese, and David Clinton, *The High-Performance Workforce Study* (Executive Summary), Accenture Consulting, 2004.

2. *Filling the Executive Bench: How Companies are Growing Future Leaders*, RHR International, 2004.

3. Robert Bandossy, *The Talent Edge*, *Workspan*, December 2001.

4. Cited in CCL e-Newsletter. Cindy McCauley, "Identify: A New View for Leading in a Diverse World." Online survey conducted by The Center for Creative Leadership, July 2005. www.ccl.org/CCLCommerce/news/newsletters/enewsletter/2005/JULjunpollresults.

5. *Filling the Executive Bench: How Companies are Growing Future Leaders*; white paper by RHR International, 2004.

6. Robert Gandossy and Tina Kao, *Channels to Anywhere: The Supply Chain for Global Talent*, Hewitt Associates, 2004.

CHAPTER 2

SELECTING THE KING'S ADVISOR

Never give a sword to a man
who can't dance.

—CELTIC SAYING

History is replete with kings who were smart enough to make use of skilled advisors. These individuals fulfilled a number of important roles. Not only were they counted upon to offer sage advice on the emerging political landscape and the changing strengths and vulnerabilities of other countries, but the king also relied upon his advisor to serve as an independent set of eyes and ears for noting and accurately interpreting the subtle intricacies of the king's court.

- Who exactly could be trusted, and who was to be carefully watched?
- Who, within the court, represented the king's interest?
- Which players were acting primarily in their self-interest?
- How were political alliances and sensitivities changing?
- What were the deeper implications of a rival leader's most recent moves?

15

In short, the king's advisor was more than just a counselor—this aide also served as a guide, a voice of reason in a divided court, a devil's advocate to present dissenting views, and (when occasion called for it) even the king's conscience.

Meet The New Advisor: The Chief Talent Officer

In the game of talent strategy, today's "kings"—our CEOs and heads of nonprofit organizations—have come to understand the wisdom of employing a new "advisor to the throne": the chief talent officer (CTO). In most organizations this individual is represented by the senior-most leader in Human Resources, organizational effectiveness or management development. While the title "chief talent officer" is sometimes applied to this individual, the role of chief talent advisor might also be represented by a variety of other titles, such as vice president of "talent management," "organizational effectiveness," or "management development." The title itself is relatively unimportant. What is important is that *who you select as your CTO and how you make use of this person are decisions that can significantly affect your ability to capture, develop, and retain exceptional leadership talent.*

If you think that I'm overstating this, please keep in mind that ten years ago, many CTOs were still relegated to the relatively innocuous task of managing the after-the-fact documentation of performance reviews on top-level executives. Over the past decade this role has quickly evolved, to the point where today's CTOs are coming to assume the role of strategic business partner whose decisions and actions can have a profound effect both on the overall strength of an organization's leadership bench, and through this, on an organization's bottom-line performance. Consider the following functions performed by today's CTO:

- To borrow a military analogy, the CTO is usually called upon to "take point" on talent strategy. This means staying ahead of developments in the field and of business changes that are impacting the organization, in order to be able to advise the CEO and senior team on the most effective direction that can be set for the company's talent management efforts. Doing this well requires the ability to keep one eye on the organization's evolving business environment, the second on anticipated changes to organizational structure, and the third (yes, good CTOs come equipped with three eyes) on how these changes are likely to alter the skill and experience composition required of the company's leaders. A good CTO will help you anticipate and plan for leadership talent issues before they arise. This might involve alerting you to how an upcoming merger will raise retention risks for certain key players, or helping you identify the talent acquisition, development, and deployment actions you will need to take to exploit an unanticipated business opportunity.

• CTOs are now expected to take the lead in setting the agenda for the annual organizational leadership talent and succession planning reviews. The manner in which your CTO manages these agendas determines whether your executives view them as simply another HR paper-drill, or as important opportunities for engaging in in-depth discussions on leadership talent.

• CTOs are typically charged with designing an organization's talent infrastructure. This includes building and managing such internal components as a company's performance appraisal, talent review, succession planning, high-potential assessment, and 360° systems. An important part of this charter includes managing such outsourced functions as executive recruiting, executive assessment, external executive coaches, on-site training, and university-sponsored advanced development programs. These decisions typically carry heavy financial risks, at times involving the investment of millions of dollars in decisions pertaining to leadership selection, development, and retention. To put this potential investment into perspective, consider that the cost for recruiting and relocating a single executive can be over $200,000 before that leader ever steps a foot in the door to begin to add value to a company. Even more important, poor decisions regarding program design and vendor selection can destroy the credibility and effectiveness of your talent management process.

• You should be able to count on your CTO to help you sniff out new talent, to make rigorous leadership assessment decisions, to direct or participate in searches for executive candidates, and to help you continually upgrade your leadership performance standards. Thus, the caliber of your CTO will directly affect the quality of your internal and external candidate pools, and the effectiveness of your selection, promotion, and succession decisions. There is an important risk factor here, since the cost of poor judgment calls in these areas is incalculable. Quite frankly, underpowered advisors can never identify or manage high-potential talent, since a mediocre talent manager can never be expected to help you identify top-notch people. In addition, because executive candidates are quick to size up the quality of a company's leadership bench by the person who is touted as leading that company's talent management efforts, the strength of your CTO will directly affect your ability to attract superior candidates to your company.

• If your senior team views your CTO as being highly credible, this individual will often be called upon to act as the impartial "voice of reason" to help executives work through conflicting points of view on such issues as the relative suitability of different leaders for promotional opportunities. A credible CTO can also help you advance an aggressive and innovative talent management agenda.

• On a related note, the type of CTO you select sends a strong *symbolic message* to the rest of your organization about what you are looking for in leadership talent. The reason is that if your CTO is going to be heavily involved in making key leadership decisions, other organizational leaders will come to view this individual as a visible model of your leadership standards. A mediocre CTO sends a message to your entire organization that your leadership standards are lax. The reverse is also true, when it comes to decisions involving the replacement of incumbent CTOs. If you replace a CTO who is widely regarded as being a passive, complacent "C" player with someone who is respected as a results-driven, strategic change catalyst, you clearly announce to your organization that your company is now playing to a new set of leadership standards.

Taking Point

A colleague of mine is the head of Human Resources and de facto CTO for a major U.S. pharmaceutical company. This organization has been wrestling with how to best respond to the strong erosion of its revenue base, following the recent elapse of a patent for a very popular medication. The resulting drop in revenue is forcing the company to undertake a radical change in its product development strategy, and quickly master the simultaneous management of a much broader pipeline of several potential new drugs, from initial research to FDA approval, production, and marketing. My colleague anticipates that this transition will soon force major structural changes in the company's research and marketing functions that will, in turn, lead to secondary changes in the types of technical and leadership competencies required of research directors, program managers, and marketing executives. By carefully considering these factors, this CTO will be able to ensure that changes in the drug development and production pipeline will be supported by changes to new leadership pipeline.

Nine Criteria for Selecting Your CTO

If it sounds as if I've placed unreasonable expectations on your CTO, I'd counter with the argument that it is better to start high and see who comes closest to meeting your standards than pay the price for undershooting. Having said that, let's consider three tools for assessing the performance capability of your current CTO, or CTO candidates. These include nine selection criteria for evaluating CTO competencies, ten questions you can ask for quickly sizing up potential or incumbent CTOs, and five key decisions that can test a chief talent officer's judgment and ability.

In my experience, there are nine criteria that a leader should meet to fill a CTO position. If you are a CEO or senior executive, consider these criteria as your "shopping list" for your next CTO. If you are currently operating as a CTO, this information may prove useful in helping you select your next direct report, or as guidelines for identifying successor candidates for your own position:

1. *Possesses the right HR skill-mix.* I have a strong bias that a CTO should have a skill-mix in human resources, and organization and management development. A graduate degree in HR, OD, or a related field is desirable, especially if the individual has relatively limited experience. These qualifications are especially important, given that the systems that the CTO will be expected to implement, such as executive assessment programs, are becoming increasingly sophisticated. As a result, the learning curve for understanding how to make the right design and selection decisions on these components is very steep, and can be very costly.

Whenever the CTO slot is filled by leaders from other functional backgrounds, usually one of three dangerous scenarios comes into play. First, talent management decisions can slow down to a crawl as the new CTO desperately tries to "get smart" about this new and rapidly changing field. Meanwhile, positions don't get filled, successor slots remain open, and your best performers are systematically picked off by competitors. Good luck. A second scenario is that the CTO tries to fake his knowledge of the field and ends up making bad hiring and promotional decisions, putting into play weak and ineffectual talent management systems. Finally, recognizing his lack of competency, the CTO may become overly dependent on the direction and advice of outside consultants. In this scenario your company ends up paying for unnecessary or overpriced services, and the consulting firm ends up attempting to direct your company's talent strategy—a very dangerous set of circumstances. In short: Don't go there! Find someone who understands the field and has proven her worth within several organizations.

2. *Is business savvy.* Now that I've made the case for picking someone with solid HR/OD/MD skills, let me offer a word of caution on placing too much emphasis on this functional expertise. Watch out for "HR purists"—managers who talk and act like academicians who are far removed from your business. Instead, look for someone who understands how talent management issues naturally unfold within your business setting. In making selection, promotion, and succession decisions, HR purists tend to place too much weight on executives' interpersonal and relationship building skills, since they have an in-depth understanding of these skill areas and are less familiar with such skills as project management or strategic thinking.

If you are looking for leaders who can take your business to the next level, then find a CTO who understands your key business drivers and who tracks those business factors that are likely to influence your future leadership requirements. Ideally, its great to get someone who has gathered at least a few years of experience outside of human resources.

3. *Is learning agile.* So let's assume that you find someone who has a solid HR background and the right business perspective. Stop and consider that during her first 90 days on the job your new CTO will have to:

- Quickly learn what drives your business and your industry.

- Perform a baseline assessment of your talent management system and identify what needs to be built, replaced, or refined.

- Become familiar with the profiles of your top executives.

Unfortunately, this person won't have the luxury of locking herself away in her office for a few months while she masters these areas. From the moment that she walks through your door she is going to be flooded with calls and e-mails from managers who are seeking advice on impending talent management decisions. At the same time, she'll need to be able to break free occasionally to manage through sudden crises, such as the loss of a key player or the need to provide coaching for those managers who are experiencing serious leadership issues. In short, you need to find someone who doesn't get lost in complexity and who can quickly learn on her feet.

4. *Has a good nose for executive talent.* It goes without saying that your CTO won't just be a designer of talent systems. This person will also be weighing in on important leadership decisions and will need to be a leader who can make well-reasoned decisions on the performance and potential of other leaders.

5. *Is nonpolitical.* All organizational environments are inherently political; there is no getting around this. The question is whether your CTO candidate is someone who can remain sensitive to, and knowledgeable about, the political realities of your organization without getting caught up in office politics. In other words, do you feel that your CTO candidate is someone who can place the interests of your organization first rather than operate from his own private agenda? At the heart of this question is whether your potential CTO is someone whom you feel you can trust, because when you come down to it, trust is the minimal ante that has to be offered up to get into the game of talent management.

6. *Is self-aware.* We all tend to judge others according to our own personal frame of values, experiences, and expectations. No matter how much we gather objective data on leaders, in the end our viewpoints are colored by our own perspectives. While your CTO can't rise above personal bias, he can compensate for it when expressing his own leadership talent recommendations. In my own case, I know that I tend to think and move fast, and that I respect people who are succinct and decisive. I'm not risk-aversive, and I tend to have little patience with executives who are immobilized by the presence of risks. Knowing these things about myself helps me separate out all of the personal baggage that I'm likely to carry into a talent leadership discussion.

Other executives have to manage different biases. They may tend to make snap judgments about leaders based on the leader's age (I've seen age bias work in both directions), marital status, university affiliation, or even their preference for sports. Does your CTO have an honest and candid "warts and all" view of her own leadership style? Can she keep personal biases in check when making delicate leadership talent decisions? That's the real question here.

7. *Has executive presence.* This is a subtlety that is often missing in CTO selection criteria. Your chief talent officer will be interfacing with your CEO and senior executive team and will need to be able to work across organizational boundaries. In addition, this person may also be called upon to represent your organization to outside interests. For example, in the past ten years I've presented to university presidents, professional and community associations, franchise owners (who can be a very confrontational group), and directing boards. So the question *you* need to ask yourself about your CTO candidate is, "Is this someone that I'd feel comfortable putting in front of our board of directors?"

A related issue is that your CTO will occasionally be called upon to give tough developmental feedback and recommendations to more senior-level leaders: namely, your CEO and senior executive team. This requires the ability to be appropriately respectful, while still being able to "have a voice in the room." Is your CTO candidate someone who can confront without appearing confrontational? Is this someone who can hold his own when coaching or advising senior-level executives?

One last facet of executive presence is that the CTO must fully understand the demands of executive work and how it differs from the work of middle managers and first-line supervisors. I have a strong bias here that it's difficult for CTOs to obtain this perspective unless they've worked at the executive level. Does your CTO candidate have corporate-wide experience at the executive level? Can your candidate "scope up" to the job, or will this person be lost in organizational complexity?

8. *Has a high tolerance for ambiguity.* Be careful of CTO candidates who tend to size up people very quickly and who sort people into simple black and white categories. These types of people tend to make snap decisions on leadership talent issues that lack depth and rigor. In contrast, during a leadership assessment or selection interview, a good CTO will go beyond the obvious questions to explore subtle and easily overlooked areas for review.

9. *Is aligned with your corporate culture.* Does your CTO represent the type of leadership style and culture that you want to build in your company, or is this person mismatched to your organizational values and leadership standards? Your ability to accurately determine the answer to this question is extremely important, because like it or not, many of your leaders will come to view your CTO as a personification of the types of leadership behavior that you wish to encourage in your company. Having said that, here are warning signs that might suggest that there is a mismatch between your CTO's leadership style and your organizational values:

- *Your organization values respect,* but your CTO talks on his cell phone or works on his Blackberry during staff meetings, or doesn't take the time to respond to voicemails or e-mails.

- *Your organization values teamwork,* but during team discussions your CTO comes across as being closed to other points of view, and continually finds herself locked into win-lose discussions.

- *Your organization values accountability,* but your CTO repeatedly misses deadlines and makes excuses for not delivering on promises.

- *Your organization values chain of command,* but your CTO functions as a "loose cannon," often making decisions without your approval or knowledge.

- *Your organization values employee development and empowerment,* but your CTO micromanages his function and doesn't push people in his department to develop their abilities.

EVALUATING A SALES DIRECTOR'S LEADERSHIP ABILITY

In my own case, several years ago while working for a previous employer, I was called upon to make an executive assessment of a newly installed sales director who had quickly established the reputation of being too aggressive and controlling. In this type of situation, it is easy to jump to conclusions after only a cursory interview with the leader's manager and immediately launch into corrective action. The problem is that if we lack a clear read on the situation, such an approach can lead to poor talent judgment calls. In this case, after taking the time to interview the director, a few of her direct reports, the director's manager, and a few peer managers, I was able to uncover some interesting contextual pieces that shed additional light on the problem:

- The leader had been brought in by senior management to raise the performance bar for her sales team, which had been having difficulty meeting the company's tough new revenue targets.

- Once hired, the sales leader immediately attempted to bring into the company a lot of new sales concepts and techniques that forced her team to rethink their sales approach. This action proved highly unpopular with her work group. It was, however, necessary because while many of these sales managers and account reps knew how to keep existing customers happy, they weren't very effective at capturing new accounts that lay outside of their core business areas.

- The new director had replaced the previous director who was terminated due to poor performance. The previous director was loved by his team because of his personable and caring leadership style. Unfortunately, another feature of this style was that he didn't force his sales managers to be accountable for their performance.

As a result of these interviews, I determined that it was true that the sales director needed coaching on how to provide performance feedback and to more effectively communicate to her team the rationale for change. On the other hand, uncovering this additional background information allowed me to reframe the sales director's actions to her manager and work team in terms of the broader business picture. Had I given in to the desire to make a snapshot judgment based on the initial interview, not only would I have formed an overly-critical picture of the sales director, but I might have also inadvertently sabotaged the change process that she was attempting to put in place.

Ten Questions You Should Pose to Your CTO

One of the best ways of testing the competency of your CTO, or CTO candidate, is to ask this individual questions that test his knowledge of the field and his ability to make well-considered talent decisions. Figure 2-1 provides ten questions that you can use in your interview process and outlines the types of information that you can obtain from each question.

Five Decisions That Test Your CTO's Judgment and Ability

If a strategist's competence is revealed by the decisions she makes, then I'd contend that there are five talent management decisions that test the capabilities of any CTO. Now, while you could simply sit back and observe what your CTO does in the following situations, that approach carries with it a heavy risk. A better option is to pose these situations to your CTO as hypothetical scenarios ("How would you respond given the following situation. . . . ?") and then see what her answers tell you about her ability to think like a talent strategist:

Critical CTO Decisions

1. *The Decision About Where to Start.* At any one time your organization will probably find itself confronted with innumerable bench-building challenges. Given this situation, the first basic decision your CTO needs to address is, "Where do we start?" While I don't have a pat answer to this question, I've found that a useful starting point is for a CTO to work with his senior executives to construct a clear picture of the organization's desired future, then compare these emerging needs with the quality and scope of the leadership strength that is currently in place to meet these challenges, and finally to construct methods and programs to close the gap between future business needs and current talent capacity. In the next chapter I'll elaborate on a six-step process for implementing this talent management approach, but for now the important point to remember is that you should be leery of any CTO who wants to launch into the creation of certain leadership develop-

Figure 2-1. Questions you should ask of your CTO.

What You Should Ask Your CTO	What These Questions Tell You
1. If you were to leave today who would you recommend to replace yourself?	• Ability to make good talent calls • Ability to look ahead 3-5 years to anticipate changing leadership needs
2. What's the biggest business challenge that you think we'll be facing over the next five years, and what do you think we need to be doing now to prepare for this challenge from a leadership perspective?	• Ability to "play point position" for the organization • Insight into your business and industry
3. What do you think about . . . (pick a top-rated, international leadership development program for review)? What are two or three programs that are comparable or better than this program?	• Ability to stay current in field • Knowledge of best practices
4. Who do you think we should select for the. . . . (name an executive function) position?	• Ability to make talent calls • Knowledge of your leadership base
5. Where do you see. . . . (name an executive) in five years? What role do you see this person playing in our company? What does she need to do to close the development gap and prepare for this role?	• Skill in high-potential assessments • Knowledge of the changing organizational landscape
6. How does our company's talent management process compare with those of our competitors?	• Ability to stay current in the field • Ability to track and poach best practices from competitors
7. How would you describe your own most important leadership development area? How do you know that this is your most important area for improvement?	• Self-knowledge • Ability to be open to feedback

8. Next week I need to present to our Board of Directors a ten-minute presentation on the subject of (pick a subject related to talent management). Could you develop this and review it with me before the meeting?	• Executive presence • Big Picture View—the ability to discuss talent management from a business perspective
9. Taking a look at the talent management infrastructure we've currently developed, where do we now need to focus our attention over the next few years? What's first on the agenda?	• Strategic thinking • Ability to align talent goals with business needs and priorities
10. If we were to make the following change to our organizational structure next year (pick one) what would be the ramifications to our leadership bench? What should we begin to plan for?	• Ability to link changing organizational structure to talent management • Ability to anticipate emerging talent management issues

ment, acquisition, and/or retention programs without having first formulated a clear picture of future leadership requirements.

2. *The Decision About Where to Focus Limited Resources.* If you think carefully about your organization, you will find that certain work groups and departments are viewed as mission crucial to success and merit a disproportionately high allotment of your company's time, staff, and attention. Quite frequently, these are functions that are in rapid transition, requiring a high degree of attention to how leaders can be deployed for greater effectiveness. If faced with the decision of resource allocation, there are several subordinate questions can be used to guide a CTO on this decision:

• What aspects of our bench are most in need of strengthening? Is there a particular division, department, management level, or function that merits special attention? In one logistics services company in which I worked, one of our "mission critical" work groups was the sales team that supported large-account management. The business argument was that our top twelve corporate accounts represented over 80 percent of our revenue base. In another company, a leader in the hotel industry, we decided to focus on our marketing function to support a badly needed ramp-up of our brand portfolio. What's hurting in your organization?

•   Another consideration involves knowing which talent functions to build internally and which to outsource. External consultants can provide a number of key specialized services, but keep in mind that there will be certain core functions over which you will want to retain ownership. For example, several very good vendor-supplied 360° multi-rater feedback programs are readily available. However, if you purchase one of these programs, who owns the competency system on which this program is based—your organization or the vendor? That's an important decision, if you intend to thread your leadership competency model through other talent management systems, such as your managerial performance appraisal system, or if you would like to retain the ability to periodically customize this competency model to your own needs.

•   You also need to consider the *sustainability* of the programs you develop. Since many talent development programs involve a three- to five-year implementation span, when making initial resource commitments to a major program you need to ask yourself whether these commitments will be sustainable over this time-period.

ALLOCATING TALENT MANAGEMENT RESOURCES

Shortly after coming on board with a financial services and insurance company, my manager called me into his office one day and asked me why I was pushing for the development of a certain management development program for two of the company's divisions. I patiently explained that I was recommending that we allocate resources to our divisions based on the comparative size of each unit's employee base. My manager went to a flipchart and sketched out the comparative employee base for each of our six divisions. Next to those figures he wrote down each unit's contribution to the corporation's overall EBITDA and revenue for the past year, as a percentage of overall corporate earnings. Finally he circled the two business units that were expected to have the highest anticipated growth rate over the next five years. The message was clear—one of our much smaller divisions contributed a huge amount to the bottom line and was expected to grow even faster over the next five years. It was this business unit that merited the lion's share of our attention.

3. *The Decision How to Intervene in a Tough Leadership Crisis.* The idea of "thinking strategically" doesn't necessarily have to equate with getting locked into a set of overly rigid and bureaucratic plans. Good talent strategists understand that many of the talent management challenges they will encounter appear suddenly without warning or precedent, and may require fast and incisive decision making. Such decision points could involve:

- What to do when a fast-rising star player suddenly jumps ship, leaving you scrambling to decide whom to put in charge of a key business initiative.

- Mediating a political tug-of-war regarding who, among several strong internal and external job candidates, should be moved into a new position or given a rare opportunity for a high-visibility development opportunity.

- Having to decide how fast you will intervene to deal with a newly hired manager whose leadership style is driving away some of your junior, high-potential talent.

Faced with these types of situations, the quality of your CTO's decision-making ability is shown not only by *what* decision is made, but also by *how* your CTO navigates through the decision process. While there are no cookie-cutter answers here, I'd contend that an effective CTO is someone who:

- Recognizes the warning signs of such problems. The voluntary termination of one good employee could mean a number of things, but if, over the course of a year, your CTO learns about several people who have fled a department and does nothing to intervene, something is wrong. The question here is how big a leadership talent problem has to get before your CTO takes note of it.

- Knows who to bring into the problem; that is, which two or three organizational stakeholders have to be brought on board, how quickly they need to be brought up to speed, and through what communication avenues (face-to-face discussions, brief phone interviews, etc.).

- Balances a willingness to uncover the relevant facts with fast decision making. Can your CTO take decisive action or does she study a problem to death?

Finally, leadership issues, such as the ones that I've described, involve a variety of response options, from the slow and subtle to the quick and heavy-handed. In the example of the abrasive newly-hired manager that I mentioned earlier, such actions can range from providing the leader's manager with feedback, to providing coaching, to moving to reposition or terminate the manager. To what degree does your CTO consider both the human impact and the business implications of sensitive leadership talent issues, and act accordingly?

UNDERSTANDING THE HUMAN AND BUSINESS IMPLICATIONS OF TALENT DECISIONS

One of my colleagues, who heads up the talent management function for a large consumer products manufacturer, once asked my advice on managing the downsizing of one of her smaller business units. The company's plan was to shed about 15 percent of their overhead costs, a move that would allow them to direct a much leaner but more profitable organization more tightly against an increasingly smaller, core market. The business rationale was good, and most of the reduction-in-force (RIF) had already been completed when the well-respected general manager of this division announced that he was leaving in a few weeks to head up another company.

My astute friend quickly gauged that this action would have an adverse affect on employee morale and might lead to another round of voluntary terminations among some of the departing GM's direct reports. She also suspected that the loss of the GM might create misgivings among the company's largest corporate customers regarding the organization's ability to meet projected performance goals.

Working together, my colleague and I mapped out a "retention risk assessment" for all critical management positions in her company. We then recommended plans for taking such actions as having senior executives meet individually with the direct reports to assure them of their job security, and putting into place retention bonuses for the best performers. My colleague and I also offered up recommendations for how one of the senior executives might coach the direct report who would be assuming the head position on an interim basis. Finally, we provided senior managers with our rationale as to why her company would probably need to go outside to find a suitable permanent replacement.

Part of this planning also involved getting the company's senior management to accept a realistic time-line that would be required to fill the GM position. This was important in order that the senior team develop a realistic assessment of how long the interim replacement might need to be at the helm of this company.

In reflecting back on this incident there was no one single decision that definitively defined my colleague's competence as a CTO. Instead, her skill was demonstrated by her ability to map out the likely course of this event, and to be able to carefully consider how all of these varied decision points needed to be simultaneously reviewed and integrated for maximum effectiveness.

4. *The Decision How to Frame the CTO Charter.* As noted earlier in this chapter, it is easy for a chief talent officer to find herself overwhelmed with a confusing array of leadership talent initiatives. What the CTO chooses to put in the center of her radar screen tells you a great deal about how this leader frames her contribution value to your organization. In my experience, high-impact CTOs focus their attention on helping senior executives think through the critical decisions that frame their talent strategy. (Chapters 4 through 7 provide a systematic way of wading through these decisions points.) In addition, effective CTOs continually search for talent management recommendations that anticipate and support emerging business initiatives. They see themselves first and foremost as business partners and advisors, and only secondarily as OD specialists, trainers, and management developers. In conclusion, one way to get a good read on your CTO's experience and competence level is ask this person how the charter for the talent management function should be framed and communicated to the rest of your organization.

5. *The Selection of Succession Candidates to the CTO's Role.* This one decision provides a wealth of information about how effectively your CTO makes judgment calls about leadership talent. Even if your CTO currently lacks a strong internal successor candi-

date, having an in-depth discussion on this subject can reveal a lot of useful information about your CTO, including:

- The degree to which your CTO is able to look forward and project out to determine how leadership requirements are likely to change over the next few years.

- Whether your CTO is able to cast a wide enough net to identify nonobvious successor candidates (leaders who are hidden away in other parts of the organization) who might not otherwise surface for discussion.

- Whether your CTO is able to gauge the performance of internal successor candidates against potential best-in-the-field external replacements.

- The performance standards your CTO has set for himself, and whether he intends to voluntarily raise the bar on these standards over the next few years.

Making the Best Use of Your CTO

Once you've made the right selection decision regarding a CTO, there are five steps that you can take to make certain that your CTO adds full value to your organization.

1. *Develop a clear charter, goals, and metrics.* As noted earlier in this chapter, it is easy for a chief talent officer to find herself overwhelmed with a confusing array of leadership talent initiatives. This, in turn, can lead to confusion among the CTO, CEO, and senior team as to the core mission and charter for the talent management function. A good way of clearing through the debris is through the use of what I refer to as the target exercise.

To complete this exercise, ask your CTO to draw a bull's-eye graphic on a flipchart (as illustrated in Figure 2-2) and then write down on separate note cards the different responsibilities that your CTO feels are a critical part of the talent management function.

Figure 2-2. Clarifying the charter of the CTO.

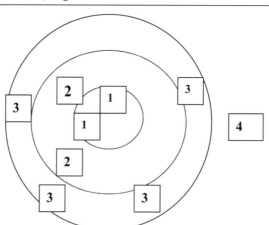

Level 1:
- Provide coaching, assessment, and placement and succession recommendations for our top corporate executives.
- Provide recommendations related to the long-term (3-5 year) upgrading of our current top leadership bench, to prepare us for the project expansion of our Alpha division.

Level 2:
- Develop a high-potential pool of our top junior executives (director-manager) and provide targeted development plans for these individuals. Assess their suitability for senior-level placements over the next five years and recommend appropriate development assignments to prepare them for these roles.
- Work with the HR department to develop supportive Talent Management infrastructure to support the hiring, development, and retention of our strongest leaders. This should include the migration of our current PM process to an enterprise-wide, online system.

Level 3:
- Design and manage additional infrastructure components to include the creation of a uniform executive assessment process, and the development of 360° review process.
- Work with the organization development function to conduct an organizational review of key functions that will require significant changes to leadership scope and function, and remap our current leadership competency models to align with these changes.
- Conduct a two-year projection of the most critical leadership talent gaps within our company by market area, product line, and corporate function, and recommend actions for closing these gaps.
- Manage partnerships with leading business schools and external consulting houses to develop a recommended management development curricula for our middle managers.

Level 4
- Develop a foundations management skills program for first-line supervisors.

Only one function should be placed on each card. Next, ask your CTO to place the cards on the flipchart, with those cards in the center representing the functions and responsibilities that she feels are most central to the CTO charter. Each successive ring implies functions that are further away from the core. Those cards placed in the outer ring (space "4") are functions that your CTO feels are only marginally related to his function. Once completed, this simple graphic serves as a great tool for gaining senior executive alignment on how priorities should be assigned to the CTO function. The same process can be used to reach agreement on how the CTO function will be successively built out over a five-year time period. Figure 2-2 shows the types of representative functions that might be included in this type of charter review.

2. *Keep your CTO close to the action.* I'd like to offer up two recommendations here. First, where your CTO is placed on your organization chart communicates a lot to your leaders about the importance your company places on talent management. It also influences the level of credibility that your CTO has with your senior team. Finally, to be able to effectively do his job, your CTO will need to have access to (and manage the control of) a great deal of sensitive information, from executive compensation to senior managers' executive assessment reports and performance appraisals. Together, these factors suggest that your CTO should report no more than two levels away from your CEO or corporate president, with the ideal situation being a direct reporting status to your CEO or corporate president. This is particularly important if your expect your CTO to be in a position to help you plan out the leadership talent you will need to meet potential business challenges, or to have the credibility needed to provide feedback and recommendations to your senior management team.

Another way to keep your CTO close to the action is to encourage this leader to get out into the field and meet regularly with your division presidents and key department heads. This is the only way for a talent leader to keep abreast of organizational issues that provide a clear reflection of leadership performance. It is also one of the best ways to help uncover emerging junior leaders in your organization. Finally, getting out into the field is the best way for your CTO to keep appraised of the changing business context that shapes leadership talent issues.

KEEPING CLOSE TO THE ACTION

In one of my previous positions I had only been working in my role as a CTO for a few months when one of our company's HR directors asked to speak to our company president about a "serious leadership issue" involving the head of our IT department. According to the HR director, she had received numerous complaints regarding the fact that the IT leader was creating a huge level of demoralization within his department. In addition, several of these complaining employees had apparently alluded to the looming threat of "wholesale turnover" in this department. Knowing this senior manager and several of the members of his work team, I found this story a little hard to swallow. Over the next day I was able to discretely contact a few individuals to find out the following:

- Only a few people in the department were actually complaining. Unknown to my director, these individuals were mediocre performers and had the reputation for being chronic whiners.

- The new IT director had been pushing his department to transform itself from a focus on such transactional services as software and hardware installation and call-desk operations, to the strategic deployment of enterprise-wide technology systems. Of the few people who had opted to leave the department over the past year, almost all were managers who were deemed not to be able to make this transition, and who had been counseled to move out of the organization. The best and the brightest performers were adjusting well to the new departmental charter.

Once again, in this situation it would have been easy to take action without first having all of the facts. However, the fact that I had previously spent a lot of time working with the managers in this department paid off well by helping me quickly sort through the data points and distill the underlying issues.

3. *Carefully position your CTO to your senior team.* It's quite likely that the CTO function may be new to your organization, or you may decide after reading this chapter that you wish to substantially alter the core charter of this function. In either case, you can increase the effectiveness of your CTO by insuring that your senior team clearly understands the role that this person is to play in your organization:

- Communicate to your team the charter, priorities, and phased implementation approach to talent management that will be undertaken by your CTO.

- Consider using your regularly scheduled executive retreats as opportunities for showcasing the activities of your talent management function.

- Explain to your team how the CTO function will share accountabilities with other HR functions. For example, which function will be responsible for coaching executives on performance problems or for managing executive assessment and recruiting?

- To assist in their on-boarding, put new CTOs in touch with experienced "mavens"—e.g., those internal leaders who are generally respected within your company as having a good understanding of the direction your company is headed, and who can provide advice regarding how proposed talent management projects are likely to "land" in your organization.

- Let your senior team know that your CTO has your confidence. Senior executives will form their own opinions about this leader based on such things as the degree to which your CTO has access to certain sensitive information on impending organizational changes, and the degree to which your CTO is invited to senior meetings.

4. *Take your CTO off the board.* Having placed your CTO "close to the action," I recommend that you consider taking her "off the board." This means positioning the CTO job as one that has no promotion potential within your organization—a terminal role. I know that this sounds a little strange, but hear me out. First, you can't get the best value from your CTO if this person is politically maneuvering for self-promotion. More importantly, if this individual is not slated for further advancement in your company, you help position her as politically neutral to the rest of your organization. Finally, consider that it is very difficult for a CTO to take hard stances on talent issues and to be willing to confront senior managers about tough leadership problems if, in the back of the CTO's mind, she feels that a year or two down the road she may be eventually reporting to one of these same senior managers. In short, the paradox here is that by taking your CTO off the board, you make her a stronger player in her own right.

5. *Feed the CTO information.* Many talent management functions, such as executive recruiting or the creation of executive development programs, require extensive lead time for design and implementation. Others, such as organizational redesign or the assessment of bench strength across business functions, require a solid grounding in the broader business context in which these changes are occurring. In these types of situations, the effectiveness of your CTO is directly related to your willingness to openly

share information on such areas as planned restructurings, M&A activity, or the (as yet unannounced) departure of a star player. Sharing this type of information well in advance allows your CTO to ask reasonable questions, obtain needed background information, understand any sensitive constraints to decision making, and plan ahead. The flip side of this is that if you don't feel comfortable sharing this kind of information, perhaps that's a sign that you have the wrong person in the job. Only work with a CTO whom you trust, and demonstrate that trust by giving this leader the information he needs to do his job effectively.

CHAPTER 3

FRAMING YOUR STRATEGY

> Perception is strong and sight weak. In
> strategy it is important to see distant things as
> if they were close and to take a distanced
> view of close things.
>
> —MIYAMOTO MUSASHI
> JAPANESE SAMURAI AND SWORD MASTER

When asked to describe how they go about developing a talent management strategy, many HR leaders tell me that they start off by attempting to identify the leadership competencies that are most important to their leaders' success. Such an answer reflects what I call an "inside-out" approach to talent management, which proceeds from an internally derived view of leadership needs, competencies, and programs. Unfortunately, while quite popular, the inside-out approach is seldom effective because it fails to fully prepare the organization to meet future business conditions.

Building Talent from the Outside-In

As is illustrated in Figure 3-1, the alternative "outside-in" approach to talent management starts out with an environmental scan to construct a clear picture of an organization's evolving business,

Figure 3-1. The outside-in approach to talent management.

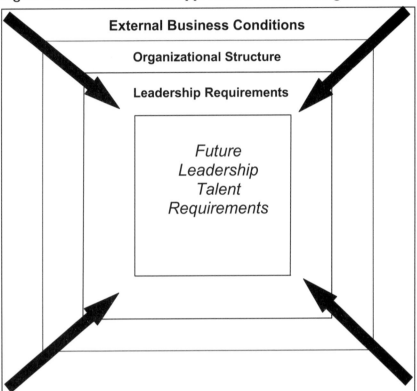

political, and economic landscape. For corporations and businesses, this means understanding the company's changing markets and competitive position. For nonprofit organizations, the outside-in approach translates into tracking changes in legislation, funding sources, or community agendas that are likely to affect the future health and growth of these agencies. In both cases, taking an outside-in approach to talent management means determining how emerging external opportunities and constraints are likely to alter the organizational structure and culture in which leaders will be called upon to perform. This approach then attempts to determine how these external and organizational changes are likely to transform leaders' roles, responsibilities, and performance standards.

Ideally, what emerges from the integration of business strategy, organizational structure, and ever-changing leadership requirements is a talent strategy that is future-focused, in that it is based on a model of how the organization's leadership bench will need to look and function three to five years down the path. *This ability to plan for the future becomes even more important the higher we climb up management ladder*, given that with each rung up the ladder it takes more time to prepare leaders for future roles. Thus, while it may take one to three years for a sales representative to progress to the role of local sales manager, it usually requires a local sales manager a longer period of time to develop the competencies and experience needed to succeed as a director of sales. In addition, at higher management levels, the talent management decisions we make involve greater risks because they exert a broader and more pervasive impact on our organizations. The point is that, as we move from management development actions directed toward front-line supervisors or middle managers, to those aimed at executive managers, it is essential that we be able to look farther down the road before formulating our talent strategy.

THE OUTSIDE-IN APPROACH IN ACTION

Years ago I worked for a jet engine manufacturer during the time that this company was attempting to make the transition from being dependent upon the U.S. military market as the sole source of its revenue, to its first entry into the commercial market. This dramatic market shift required a radical redefinition in the roles required of the company's marketing and sales professionals, many of whom were ex-military personnel, whose sales experience had been limited to preparing proposals and demonstrations for the U.S. military. Those managers who couldn't make the transition had to be replaced, while others required extensive development. This is but one example of the types of large-scale

> environmental shifts, such as changes to business condi-
> tions, mergers, and acquisitions, or a company's first entry
> into international markets, that require organizations to
> adopt very different expectations of their leaders.

Figure 3-2 provides a recommended six-step approach to talent management that proceeds from identifying future business needs, to assessing emerging leadership challenges and talent gaps, and planning actions for closing those gaps. I have found that this model can serve as a useful roadmap, not only for sorting through competing talent management priorities, but also for communicating to senior managers the process that you intend to follow for integrating your company's business strategy with your talent management strategy. As you read through the following section, try to use this map to plot where your organization currently is in its organizational development efforts.

Step One: Identify Future Requirements

The first step involves understanding where your organization is headed, both in terms of its long-term goals and any emerging opportunities and constraints in your marketplace and industry that could seriously affect your organization's future growth. The "opportunities and constraints" to which I'm referring are those changes in your marketplace, customer base, competitors, and regulatory environment that will play the greatest role in transforming your competitive field of play. In my own area, the media industry, some of the changes that I try to track are:

- The continued integration of Internet, print, broadcast, and cable, a move which is forcing many journalists to rethink their approaches to the creation of news content, and

Figure 3-2. The six steps of talent.

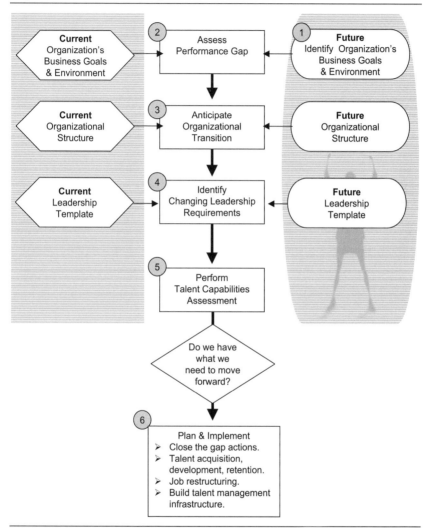

which is offering sales leaders new opportunities for cross-platform selling.

- The rapid expansion of televised commercials as a part of in-store marketing—a move that opens up new advertising markets to both broadcast and cable companies.

- The aging of the U.S. population, and the changing media preferences for this audience.

- The challenge of retaining the viewership and readership of a younger audience, one that wasn't weaned on television and newspapers.

- The rapid growth in ethnic diversity in the United States, with particular attention to the expanding Hispanic consumer market.

- The incredible fragmentation of the customer market, not only through the introduction of hundreds of new alternative channels, print advertisers, and Web-based marketing, but through the intrusion of newer forms of media, such as satellite television, video and online gaming, and the entrance of new wireless competitors into the field.

- The introduction of VOD, or voice-on-demand, which allows viewers to skim past commercials, and which will force innovation in media advertising.

Given the rapid pace of change, the challenge you face is not only tracking those emerging trends that are shaping your own industry, but also anticipating their potential impact on your company. While you could attempt to arrive at these answers by studying up on your company's written strategic plan and annual reports, a more effective technique is to engage your CEO and senior team in discussions about how they view your organization's future. This approach offers the following advantages:

- Your senior leaders may feel that your company's long-term strategic plan is still in the stage of preliminary development, and that it is not yet ready to be formally presented to employees in your organization. At the same time, they might be far enough down the path to feel comfortable engaging you in an informal discussion on your company's overall direction, and the emerging trends that are shaping your industry.

•   You will often find that what emerges from these discussions is not a clear path to the future, but rather a labyrinth of options through which the best minds in your organization are attempting to navigate. In the very act of dialoguing on this subject, sometimes you can help other executives develop and detail their own thinking in these areas, so that everyone comes away with a clearer sense of future opportunities and challenges.

•   Even when these conversations don't provide you with a clear sense of where your organization is headed, they often tell you what will become *less important* in the future, and where your organization is likely to see less of a continued return for its investment of talent resources.

Figure 3-3 illustrates the types of questions you can pose to your executives to obtain a clearer picture of your organization's future direction.

USING EXECUTIVE DIALOGUE TO GAUGE FUTURE DIRECTION

While I was working for one former employer, it became obvious in discussions with the CEO and senior team that these executives believed the company was losing money on its European operations. The company was clear that over the next three years it would pull back from all but a few "gateway" cities, such as London and Paris, and even in these areas it would come to depend more on co-branding arrangements with international partners to maintain its presence. This piece of information proved valuable in helping me plan out the level of leadership development resources that needed to be allocated to the support of our international teams.

Figure 3-3. Questions that frame future focus.

Over the next few years . . .

1. From where will our revenue growth come? What aspects of our business are most likely to significantly grow, diminish, or evolve?
2. What work functions, products, and divisions will provide the engine for this growth?
3. What organizational areas are likely to become less critical to our future direction? Where might we expect additional reductions-in-force or outsourcing to take place?
4. When we look at the leadership talent we now have in place in these areas, how would we evaluate our talent capacity? Where are our greatest talent gaps? Where are we at risk?
5. How broad and deep is our current talent pipeline for meeting future demands? Do we have in place now the people we need to do business tomorrow? If not, what's the impact on our business?
6. In what functions is the market supply for leadership talent likely to become a critical issue? What implications will these changes have for our executive compensation and development systems?
7. When we look at our five-year forecast for hiring—and our projected attrition through retirement and turnover—what do we see happening to our leadership pipeline? Will our bench become weaker or stronger?
8. What are we currently doing to supplement our leadership pipeline? Is it working? How do we know?

Step Two: Assess Performance Gaps

The next step involves assessing the most significant gaps in your organization's current performance, and how you will need to strengthen that performance in order to help the organization achieve its future direction. At this stage, *try to avoid jumping ahead to predict how these changes are likely to influence your leadership talent mix.* Instead, simply focus on identifying potential changes to the overall performance of your organization. Here are a few examples:

• One logistics services company found that their biggest projected change involved expanding from North America into Latin

America. The performance challenges their organization faced were the lack of prior experience in marketing to the Latin American market, and the need to quickly understand the unique distribution networks that were a necessary part of this transition.

• For a hotelier, the change involved evolving from a company that owned and managed all of its assets, to becoming a leaner, pure-play franchiser (a situation in which all properties are owned and operated by franchise owners).

• A U.S. insurance company with which I had previously worked recognized that its biggest performance challenge involved making the transition from being a provider of traditional insurance services, to marketing and selling a diversified portfolio of investment options.

• I know of a leading U.S. business school whose student population is increasingly characterized as middle-aged professionals who are undergoing mid-career transitions. These individuals are looking for flexible instructional formats that can make them more marketable to future employers. As a result, the university is attempting to evolve from its dependence on "bricks and mortar" to become an "online, anytime" university.

When you look out into the next five years, what are the most important, broad-scale performance changes that will be required of your own organization?

Step Three: Anticipate Organizational Transitions

At this point you may think that you're ready to try to identify the size and skill composition of the leadership bench you'll need to close these gaps. The problem, however, is that you're still missing one important piece of the puzzle, which is identifying potential changes to your organizational structure. You see, *organizational structure serves as the bridge that links business strategy to leadership requirements.*

In making this last statement, I mean that before a company can set out upon a new path, be it launching a new product, expanding into new geographical territory, or attempting to capture a new customer base, it has to first make significant changes in how its business functions are organized. These changes may involve modifications to functional charters or reporting structures, the creation of entirely new organizational units such as new product development teams, or the centralization or decentralization of certain organizational functions. They can also include such sweeping, enterprise-wide reorganization efforts as the integration of different organizations through mergers, acquisitions, or business partnerships.

It's easy to feel overwhelmed when you set out to construct a clearer picture of the changes that your own organization is likely to face over the next few years. Since almost every aspect of your organization may be touched by these changes, how can you go about focusing on those areas that are most important to talent management? My recommendation is to start out by working with your senior managers to identify those business units and departments that, as a result of anticipated revenue growth or their strategic market position, are likely to play a more critical role in your company's future success. Then drill down a level and ask your senior executives to help you identify the most mission-critical leadership positions within each of these organizational units. By "mission-critical" I'm referring to those positions that, if left unfilled for a prolonged period of time or headed up by weak leaders, can seriously impede your company's performance. This approach, as simple as it may seem, encourages executives to step away from discussions of individual leaders and focus in on the business impact of the evolving organizational structure.

OUTSOURCING AS AN ORGANIZATIONAL TRANSITION

A few years ago I headed up the talent management function for a company that was attempting to offshore and outsource over 3,000 customer service jobs (20 percent of its employee base) to India. Unfortunately for the company, at the time that I came on board it was well past the "honeymoon phase" of its outsourcing transition, and had begun to realize that this transition would not be as easy and "turn-key" as it had been originally sold to the senior executive team.

From a talent management perspective, this organizational transition required leaders in the customer service department to move away from the day-to-day management of customer service activities. Instead, the focus for these leaders became providing technology transfer to the outsource provider, working with the IT department to build the IT infrastructure needed to support these changes, working with me and the president of the outsourcing operation to develop plans for the hiring and training of managers and employees at three sites in India, and learning to manage quality and cost control through the construction of detailed service level agreements. At the same time, on the home front this adjustment meant dealing for the first time with a massive, phased, reduction-in-force, while attempting to retain key players who needed to be kept on board through the eighteen-months retention cycle.

To make things more interesting, halfway through this transition we experienced the events of 9/11, a situation which forced us to completely reevaluate how employees in the outsourced company could best be hired, trained, and evaluated.

Armed with this information, try to identify on your organizational chart any departments or functions that represent what I refer to as *black holes, whirlpools,* and *red zones.* These are three different types of organizational dysfunctions that, if left unmanaged, can seriously weaken a company's bench strength.

Red Zones

Red zones are those organizational units in your company that, during the next few years, will require your leaders to develop entirely new skill sets and knowledge bases and to adapt to radically different performance standards. An example would be a department that, for the first time, is given responsibility for a top-line revenue function, including account generation and management, and revenue forecasting. In many cases, adapting to a red zone requires leaders to be willing to adopt very different mind-sets to their approach to work. What is involved in "adopting a different mind-set"? Quite often this means accepting the fact that in a volatile and ever-changing work environment, some of the assumptions that we've long held dear regarding the "best way" to approach our work, no longer apply. For example:

• A hotelier that attempts to switch from a business model based on hotel ownership and management, to one based on pure-play franchising has to make the mental transition from viewing the corporate office as a controlling management function, to viewing it as a supportive business partner for a group of semi-independent franchisers.

• When making the move from selling advertising via print, broadcast, or cable, to selling advertising via the Internet or wireless, an advertising sales manager must totally rethink what constitutes "value added" to customers.

• As a final example, consider what happens when certain high-volume transactional services, such as information on sick leave or 401k accounts, are outsourced or shifted to automated self-serve systems. In this situation, HR leaders must learn to quickly make the transition from focusing on transactional services, to focusing on broader HR issues that impact long-term business performance.

In each of these cases, adapting to a red zone means more than just adding on additional leadership competencies. It means that leaders have to be willing to reframe their roles and the organizational value provided by their functions. In this respect, *learning agility* becomes a critical leadership meta-competency.

There are several steps you can take to manage organizational red zones. First, pay far more attention to workforce forecasting. Learn to quickly develop at least a rough approximation of what you may need over the next few years in terms of projected leadership bench strength (the numbers and skill composition of required leaders). Although you probably won't have a detailed grasp of your headcount requirements, you can use past experiences to provide a rough estimate.

In one company in which I worked we used a well-known product launch—let's call it the "Alpha Project"—as our benchmark metric. Thus, we could tell our senior team that a new product launch might equate to "two Alphas" in terms of projected leadership requirements throughout the first two years of the project. You will also have to decide whether you will be able to take the time to develop needed leadership requirements, or if you are better served by engaging in the wholesale importing of talent from other company units or the external job market. (Additional details for managing this type of "make/buy" decision are provided in Chapter 4.)

Black Holes

Black holes are organizational areas known to hoard talent (leaders may enter these zones but never leave). One of the reasons for this is that black holes are very insular, and frequently geographically isolated, organizational units that tend to be impermeable to other parts of the organization. That is, the managers of these units erect strong territorial barriers to block the interorganizational exchange of information, ideas, and leadership talent. One of the primary difficulties in managing leadership talent within a black hole is that it is difficult to know where exceptional leaders reside in such units, and to obtain a clear, unfiltered assessment of their performance. To overcome this difficulty, consider making use of the following techniques *to obtain a clear line-of-sight to junior-level managers*:

• Create cross-functional and project teams to increase junior managers' visibility to senior-level executives,

• Supplement data from performance appraisals with the use of 360° feedback reviews, leadership assessment centers, and psychological assessments by independent I/O psychologists (psychologists who hold doctorate degrees from APA recognized programs in Industrial and Organizational Psychology). When using 360° feedback, strive to maintain some control in the selection of feedback providers, to ensure that you obtain feedback from key stakeholders rather than from close friends and cronies. These tools afford some means of independently auditing talent and locating star performers.

• To gain direct exposure to junior-level managers, create high-potential pools (more on this in Chapter 5) and make the ability to identify and sponsor candidates for such programs a criterion in the performance evaluation of senior executives.

• Encourage your senior managers to initiate informal lunch-and-learn forums with junior-level managers from different areas, or "skip interviews" in which they meet directly with junior-level managers to discuss their career goals and assess their knowledge of key business issues.

• It may be that you direct a field support function such as Human Resources, IT, or finance, that reports up to both a divisional general manager and to a corporate department with dotted-line authority over this function. If this is the case, consider using what I call cross-threading to obtain a more balanced view of your managers' leadership performance and potential. Cross-threading involves incorporating feedback from both divisional and corporate sources into your managers' annual performance appraisals, reviews of leadership potential, or 360° reviews. Figure 3-4 illus-

Figure 3-4. The use of cross-threading to assess the potential of HR leaders.

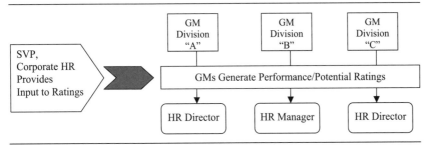

trates the cross-threading technique applied to a human resources function.

- Internal biases, such as evaluations that are based in part on personal friendships and alliances, are likely to surface within any work setting. To control for such bias, I recommend that you outsource to a reliable outside consulting firm at least part of your executive assessment process, such as the administration of your 360° process, psychological testing, or the use of independent "upgrading" interviews. Taking this step provides you with another set of checks-and-balances in your executive review process.

Whirlpools

Whirlpools are the most turbulent and stressful parts of your organization, which can easily submerge all but the most tenacious leaders. While you might argue that this description could characterize 90 percent of your company, whirlpools are most likely to be found in those areas of your organization in which:

- There is an inordinately high amount of sick leave.
- Employees voice widespread complaints about tension, stress, and burnout.
- There is an extremely high, and rapidly increasing, turnover rate.

- Employees are working extremely long hours.

- Leaders must contend with an incessant level of unpredictable and highly disruptive change. (In these situations, you may hear employees comment that it's impossible for them to stop and catch their breath before being dragged under by the next change wave.)

- Executives and managers privately voice the view that the company unit or department is in utter chaos, with leaders confused as to how to divide their time among competing, long-term goals and priorities.

Once again, within this type of work setting the leadership competency of learning agility is extremely important. Equally important is the leadership competency of resiliency, and the ability to manage uncertainty and ambiguity. Look for leaders who don't get lost in complexity, who are adept at mobilizing people to manage disruptive change, and who can develop tight agendas and clearly communicate their priorities. The simple fact is that managers who require paint-by-the-numbers work environments don't usually survive very long when dropped into whirlpools.

When attempting to conduct talent management programs within whirlpools, two things have to be kept in mind. First, in this type of high-change environment you will seldom have clear visibility into the future, and will need to make frequent adjustments to your talent management goals and resource plans. Given this constraint, restrict your planning to the short-term and keep it flexible. Accordingly, don't waste months attempting to engage in long-term, incremental programs. Forget about creating detailed leadership competency models and job descriptions, or designing multiyear leadership development programs. Instead, when you find yourself trapped in a whirlpool you'll discover that talent management takes the form of triage, through such actions as helping executives quickly fill leadership openings, or spotting the most expedient retention issues. A second, related consideration is that the senior executives who head up such organizational units are typically overwhelmed. You can help them a great deal by taking the time to ask hard questions that force them to think through their talent management priorities. Then get them to focus on those few critical actions that are both feasible, and that are likely to yield immediate payoffs in improved leadership performance.

Step Four: Identify Changes to the Leadership Template

Up to this point you've attempted to paint a clearer picture of your company's future direction, have taken a look at the ways in which your organization will need to adapt to meet future challenges, and have identified performance gaps between this future state and current organizational performance. Your next step involves constructing a model or template of how your leaders currently function, and comparing this model with a future leadership template—one that identifies the biggest changes to leaders' future roles, responsibilities, required management and technical competencies, and work experiences.

An example comes from the university that was mentioned earlier in this chapter, which has been attempting to shift from classroom to online instruction. The executive who heads up the HR function for this university tells me that the biggest leadership challenge she faces isn't finding instructors who know how to design and deliver online instruction. Instead, it is finding department heads who can provide strong "thought leadership" to guide the university in anticipating and addressing the unique resource and marketing challenges posed by the rapid expansion of such programs.

In a similar fashion, in planning for the next three to five years you may come to realize that your leaders will be called upon to develop entirely new sets of competencies and work experiences, such as:

- Developing unique technical skills (knowledge of Sarbanes-Oxley regulations, or Six Sigma methodology)
- Adapting to changes to leadership scope (the numbers of people and complexity of functions that will report to a given position)
- Assuming responsibility for a discrete profit and loss function
- Assuming responsibilities for managing customer account activities
- Becoming accountable for key work processes and systems

In addition to these changes, organizations occasionally eliminate entire organizational levels as a means of accelerating decision making, focusing accountability, and reducing headcount costs. When this happens, managers often find that certain key promotional rungs have been eliminated from their career ladders, resulting in situations in which they are called upon to master larger, more challenging developmental "jump points" in order to be considered ready for the next promotional opportunity.

UNDERSTANDING THE TALENT MANAGEMENT IMPACT OF ELIMINATING LEADERSHIP LEVELS

Some time ago I worked as an OD consultant to a U.S. manufacturing company. As part of a corporate reorganization effort, we eliminated all senior sales director positions, with the result that sales directors now reported directly to their vice presidents of sales. As a byproduct of this change, sales directors were no longer able to use the senior director position as a developmental bridge to the VP position.

Instead, they now had to master a broader range of skills in order to prepare for their next promotions. At the same time, the elimination of the position of senior sales director meant that each VP now had a much bigger job scope, in terms of larger revenue targets, a broader array of customers, and the management of a larger number of direct reports.

As a result, directors who wanted to eventually be considered for promotion to vice president had to step up to jobs that were now much larger, more complex, and in which the risk of failure was far greater for the company. This organizational change automatically eliminated some directors for promotional consideration. For the rest, the challenge we faced was developing a thorough testing and evaluation process (more on this later in the chapter) that could give the company a clear indication of who could make the leap to the next level.

Step Five: Perform a Talent Capabilities Assessment

Armed with your template or model of how leaders will need to evolve over the next few years, you are now in a position to perform a talent capabilities assessment. This assessment attempts to pinpoint the gaps that exist between your future business challenges, and the size and strength of the leadership bench you currently have in place to meet those challenges. There are two steps to developing a talent capabilities assessment.

The first step is to evaluate each of your individual leaders in terms of their assessed performance and potential. There are a number of tools available for evaluating leadership performance and potential, including performance appraisal data, 360° feedback, feedback and ratings from leadership assessment centers, psychological assessments that provide an evaluation of intelligence and personality, and assessment ratings generated by small teams of senior-level executives. Chapter 6 compares the respective advantages and disadvantages of these approaches (refer to Figure 6-3) and outlines suggested guidelines (refer to Figure 6-4) for their implementation.

Perhaps the most important thing to consider when attempting to assess leadership performance and potential is to take the time to clearly define the criteria you will use for evaluating these dimensions. Most organizations adhere to the use of clearly defined written performance standards. However, I frequently find that organizations are less clear in articulating their standards for leadership potential. Here are several useful criteria that I've seen applied to this assessment area:

- The individual's ability to advance in two or more levels in the organization.

- The ability to assume responsibility for a broader range of management responsibilities.

- The ability to "think at the next level" and interpret business decisions within a broader business context.

- The degree of learning agility displayed by the individual, as demonstrated by the leader's ability to quickly adapt to change, to interface effectively with very different types of people, and to "learn on the run." (A useful tool for assessing learning agility is the e-Choices® multi-rater feedback instrument provided by Lominger, Inc.)

The second step involves performing an evaluation of your overall leadership bench to determine the relative strength of each organizational function, department, and operating unit. While many organizations now use some version of the famous 9-grid Potential/Performance matrix to evaluate individual leaders, and to graphically show how leadership strengths vary by organizational unit, this technique still leaves open some area for confusion regarding the definition of "leadership potential." Some executives define potential in terms of a leader's potential to advance within the same functional area, while others define potential in terms of a leader's ability to assume more diverse roles across the organization. One way to minimize this confusion is to make use of the 2D Model of Leadership that is shown in Figure 3-5.

This approach requires evaluators to assess leaders in terms of both their potential to gain in scope or advance in levels (noted as the vertical axis on Figure 3-5), as well as the degree to which they have the potential to take on different kinds of organizational roles. The example shown in Figure 3-5 compares the potential of

Figure 3-5. The "2D" model of leadership potential.

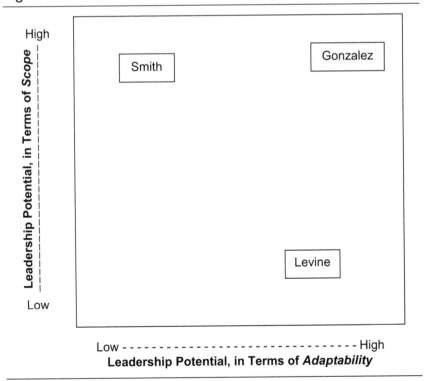

three leaders in the accounting department, who we'll refer to as Smith, Levine, and Gonzalez.

• Smith is a CPA who has a BA and an MBA in accounting. She has ten years of experience as an accountant and accounting manager, all of which have been within the same department of our hypothetical company. She is a strong leader who is viewed by her senior executives as being someone who could easily advance two levels in her function, but who would have difficulty contributing beyond this rather narrow career niche.

• Levine is a finance manager who has a BA in accounting and an MBA with a major in finance. He worked for a large accounting consulting firm for two years before moving on to a role as a valuation manager for an investment banking firm. For the past five years he has worked for our hypothetical company, first for two years in a corporate audit role, and then for another three years in the accounting and finance departments. His manager feels that while he could eventually make it to the next level of management, he would have difficulty working beyond that level. Levine could, however, perform well within a number of functions, so for that reason he is rated high in "adaptability."

• Gonzalez is a CPA who also has a BA in finance and an MBA in accounting management. Over the past seven years she has advanced quickly within a number of operations, working as an accountant, financial analyst, business development manager, and divisional controller—within both corporate functions and divisional units. She receives high marks from her managers in her ability to take on new responsibilities and lead and develop exceptional teams. As you can see in Figure 3-5, she is rated high by her managers in terms of having potential for broader scope and for being able to readily adapt to different functions.

Apart from plotting a leadership bench in terms of performance and potential, a talent capabilities assessment can also include feedback on a number of metrics, which can be used to generate an overall picture of the health of a given leadership bench. These metrics are discussed in detail in Chapter 10.

Step Six: Design and Implement "Close the Gap" Actions

The final step involves developing more sophisticated systems to track, develop, and acquire talent, such as building long-term partnerships with business graduate schools and executive recruiters, or developing succession planning, leadership talent reviews, and formal development programs. The next four chapters provide step-by-step guidelines for thinking through five key talent management decisions points, as well as the comparative trade-offs that are associated with the use of eight different talent management strategies. These talent decisions and strategies are summarized in the next chapter, within Figure 4-1.

Putting It All Together

Figure 3-6 shows how a talent strategist might incorporate the six-step method to develop a plan for strengthening the leadership bench within a company's procurement department. You can use this type of chart to engage the other members of your executive team in discussions on talent management strategy. By incorporating their feedback into a composite talent management model, you can identify those steps on which your executives are aligned on talent strategy, and those where they hold very different views regarding such areas as performance gaps or the need for organization redesign. In this way, a talent summary chart can serve as a "straw man" for encouraging your executive team to articulate the assumptions they hold about important talent management initiatives.

Figure 3-6. Integrating business and talent strategy for a newly formed strategic alliances team.

Step 1	Step 2	Step 3	Step 4	Step 5	Step 6
Identify Organization's Future Goals & Environment	**Assess Performance Gap**	**Anticipate Organizational Transition**	**Identify Changing Leadership Requirements**	**Perform Talent Capabilities Assessment**	**Implement Closing the Gap Actions**
Over the next three years our procurement department is expected to transform into a true Strategic Alliance (SA) function, which will involve the formation of long-term partnerships with key national vendors.	Our biggest performance gaps center around the lack of leadership experience in managing co-branding arrangements, and in developing branding and contracting support to secure these arrangements. In addition, currently our procurement process is fragmented and lacks uniformity. Currently, less than 5% of our revenue base is derived from such partnerships. Our goal is to raise this to 10%.	The procurement department will be reorganized to assume functions beyond materials purchasing. These will include developing co-branding and incremental revenue opportunities with such partners as credit card companies.	Our leaders in the new SA department will require skills in: • Creating strategic partnerships with key vendors. • Selling these new revenue-generating partnership opportunities to our franchise base. • Managing a discrete P&L function. • Identifying minority vendors to support our corporate diversity initiative.	We've determined that we will need to upgrade leadership talent within seven department positions to meet these requirements.	• Direct management recruiting efforts at candidates who have these skills. • Fold these new leadership requirements into the assessment criteria for succession and promotion candidates. • Conduct an in-depth internal interview process to determine the degree to which incumbent managers have these skills.

CHAPTER 4

EVALUATING STRATEGIC TRADE-OFFS

No trumpets sound when the important
decisions of our life are made.
Destiny is made known silently.

—AGNES DE MILLE, CHOREOGRAPHER

I would argue that all strategies are defined by the decisions they encompass. The trick here is not just in making superior decisions, but also in learning how to identify, from the plethora of leadership talent decisions that confront you at any moment, those few decisions that shape the events around you. I am sure that as a company executive or CTO you may have recently found yourself confronted with a number of difficult talent management decisions:

• Do I take a risk and promote this strong high-potential manager into that general manager position, or backfill with the other candidate who has far greater experience, but less long-term potential for advancement?

• Given the fact that I can only afford to send one of my ten managers to a special development workshop, who should go?

67

• Now that one of my best people has suddenly left her job, do I backfill with an internal candidate who has similar skills and experience, or conduct an external search for someone with a totally different profile?

• Should I attempt to identify individual successors to key positions, or develop a pool of candidates who could serve in a variety of positions?

• Which of the leaders in my group have the strongest potential to take on broader responsibilities within our company?

When faced with these types of talent management decisions, talent strategists and tacticians employ very different decision-making styles. Tacticians tend to treat each talent decision as an isolated occurrence. The decision to launch a new leadership development program or to find the best candidate for a position is made without referring back to the overall talent game plan. The problem with this approach is that, over time, the consequences of these isolated decisions may work against each other, producing a talent strategy that is fragmented and ineffective.

In contrast to this, like the best chess players, talent strategists are able to think several steps ahead in the game. They consider each decision within the overall context of their overarching strategy and the long-term pay-offs and pitfalls that are associated with alternative choices.

So how do talent strategists do this? In my experience, they tend to employ six guidelines to navigate through extremely complex talent management decisions:

Guideline 1: Clearly Define Your Talent Management Objectives

I know that your overall goal is to strengthen your leadership bench, but take a minute to ask yourself a few questions that can help you more carefully frame this goal:

• Do I need to make an urgent turn-around in the performance of my company?

• Am I trying to bring on board the kinds of leaders who can guide my organization through a difficult transition, such as a merger or an aggressive push into a new market?

• Am I hoping to initiate retention efforts to stem the loss of my best people?

• Am I looking for leaders who can help my organization approach its business challenges from a completely different perspective?

• Do I want to build greater talent diversity so that my leadership ranks more accurately reflect the communities I serve?

What do you hope to gain from your organization's talent management efforts? What objectives clearly capture these intentions? Are the members of your executive team aligned on importance of these objectives?

Guideline 2: Identify Those "Critical Few" Talent Management Decisions That Shape Your Strategy

Not all decisions are equally important. Certain decisions hold widespread ramifications for corporate performance in that, once enacted, they set into motion the next logical moves on the board. As I'll explain shortly, the decision to leverage most of your available resources against a few high-potential leaders (the *capstone* strategy) leads you down a very different path from the alternative decision to disperse your resources across your overall leadership bench (the *foundation* strategy). By focusing on the few decisions that guide the bulk of their decision making, talent strategists avoid becoming overwhelmed by decisions. Instead, they attempt to target those few critical decisions that can help them frame their strategy.

The five talent management decisions summarized in Figure 4-1 (more on these later in the chapter) are some of the most important decisions that talent strategists must address. What other critical talent decisions are likely to shape the leadership talent strategy of your organization?

Guideline 3: Understand the Assumptions on Which You Base Your Most Critical Talent Decisions

Talent decisions are always built upon a variety of underlying assumptions. Examples include:

• Emerging business and operating conditions ("Our core market is going south, and it looks like there may be lean times ahead for the next few years.")

• The business priorities set by your CEOs and senior management team ("Given that our company president has repeatedly focused on the need to strengthen our international performance, this is likely to be an area where I need to shore up our leadership bench.")

• Assumptions regarding the changing external market for talent ("Everything I'm reading appears to be suggesting that we're approaching a tightening of the market for mid-level IT leaders.")

Talent strategists differ from ineffective decision makers in three respects: one, they explicitly identify and spell out the assumptions that shape their decisions; two, they frequently take these assumptions out for self-review; and three, they are willing to alter their strategies based on new information. Strategists recognize that by explicitly identifying the assumptions that guide their thinking, they are better able to continually adapt their strategies to changing circumstances. In this chapter you'll be introduced to some of the assumptions that influence talent management decisions. As you encounter these examples, try to identify those few key assumptions that inform your own talent strategy, then look for ways to test the validity of these assumptions.

What assumptions do you hold that, if changed, would force you to significantly alter your talent management strategy?

Guideline 4: Acknowledge Tough Trade-Offs

Strategists understand that each talent decision involves tough tradeoffs involving the allocation of limited time, resources, and attention. In other words, they recognize that they can't do everything. The decision to pursue certain talent management efforts means being willing *not* to pursue other short-term objectives and opportunities. Thus, the decision to implement a "trade-up strategy" (see Figure 4-1) tends to be very costly and disruptive to an organization. One pursues this decision with the knowledge that a lot of money will have to be placed on the table over a one to two-year time period for the chance of capitalizing on long-term goals. The implication is that once this decision is in play, other options, such as the choice to invest in a costly leadership development workshop, may have to be postponed or eliminated.

As you read through this chapter, think about some of the talent decisions that you want to put into place. Next, make a list of those initiatives that you are willing to put on hold or remove from consideration in order to act on these key talent decisions.

Guideline 5: Employ Heuristic Decision Making

Heuristics are simple decision rules that help guide decision making under conditions of complexity, uncertainty, and continual change. Good decision makers know that asking the right questions can help them cut through confusion and get to the heart of a problem. An interesting example comes from the field of medical

Figure 4-1. Mapping the five major talent decisions.

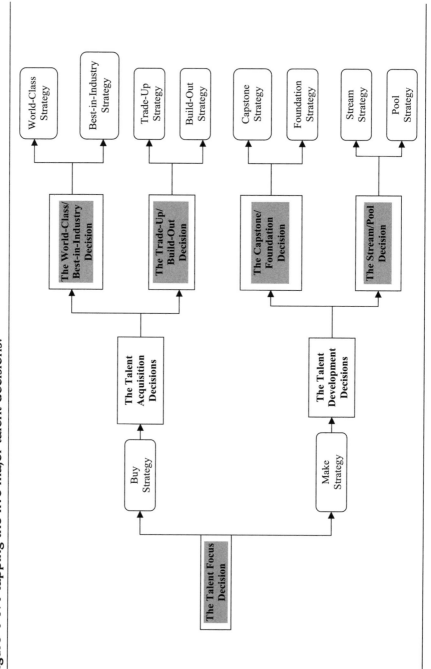

research on heart attacks. Recent research has shown that by asking patients three questions in a specified order, doctors in emergency wards can dramatically improve their chances of making a correct call on whether a patient is experiencing a heart attack. The researchers who have explored this area of study have been able to convert patients' answers to these questions into simple decision rules that can be used to guide the attending physicians.[1]

As a talent strategist you need to uncover those rules of thumb that can help you stay focused when you are facing a continually changing array of business decisions. For example, when challenged to build up the bench strength for senior-level executives, I tend to adhere to the decision rule that it's usually faster to build the bench through acquisition (hiring) than to grow the bench through development. The reason for this is the lengthy preparatory period required for someone to make the shift from tackling functionally-related problems, to addressing complex business problems at the level of general manager. However, this rule of thumb tends to be less true as one moves down the leadership ladder. As a result, when we are talking about building the bench strength for first-line supervisors, it might be a toss-up as to which route is the fastest. In Chapters 5 to 7, I will be introducing a few additional rules of thumb that you can use to guide your leadership talent decisions.

What rules of thumb guide your own decision-making process when it comes to talent decisions? As you read through the remainder of this chapter, be on the look out for additional heuristics that might be applicable to the talent decisions you are facing.

Guideline 6: Recognize the Symbolic Significance of the Talent Decisions You Make

Because organizational leaders embody the values and direction of their corporations, the talent decisions that they make hold important symbolic messages for their employees and external stakeholders. The decision to move key internal managers into a department is likely to be interpreted by others as a signal that senior managers view that function as becoming increasingly important. In the same way, the decision to fill executive openings across the organization from external applicants rather than internal candidates may be interpreted as a sign that current managers are not viewed as being strong enough to meet the business challenges that lie ahead. Talent strategists are sensitive to the symbolic nature of such talent decisions and they make their choices accordingly.

Think about some important talent management actions that were recently taken by your own organization. What subtle, symbolic messages did these actions send to your leaders?

The Five Key Decisions That Drive Talent Strategy

As I've suggested, strategic decision making involves isolating from all potential decisions you face those few that establish the field of play. For talent strategists, this boils down to understanding the impact of the following five key decisions, which are summarized in Figure 4-1.

1. *The Talent Focus Decision.* This decision, also known as the "make/buy decision," asks, "Should we rely on internal development and assessment programs (Make) or external recruiting efforts (Buy) to grow our leadership bench?" The make/buy decision is listed as the first decision in the talent decision tree (Figure 4-1) because the decision to focus on either internal development or the external acquisition of talent is one of the prerequisite choicepoints that shape the overall talent management process. This decision will be explored further in Chapter 5.

2. *The Talent Development Decisions.* Organizations that choose to focus their efforts on internal development must address two critical development decisions, which are reviewed in detail in Chapter 6.

- *The Capstone/Foundation Decision*: Should we pursue a "capstone strategy" that focuses our talent development efforts on our strongest high-potential candidates, or opt for a "foundation strategy" and spread our talent development efforts across the broader base of our leadership bench?

- *The Talent Stream/Talent Pool Decision:* Should we rely on the *talent stream* strategy of identifying individual successors for targeted positions, or focus on identifying *pools* of managers who have the potential to perform across a variety of positions?

3. *The Talent Acquisition Decisions.* Companies that choose to focus their leadership talent efforts on the external acquisition of talent are faced with two key decisions, which are discussed in Chapter 7:

- *The Trade-Up or Build-Out Decision:* Is our major hiring goal to quickly broaden our talent pipeline with talent similar to what we already have in place (the build-out strategy), or to significantly upgrade our talent bench with higher-caliber performers (the trade-up strategy)?

- *The World-Class or Best-in-Industry Decision:* In seeking out external candidates, are we better off looking for the best performers from within our industry, or should we invest the additional time and cost in importing world-class leaders from across different industries?

There are two reasons I'm encouraging you to spend time examining these five talent management decisions. First, by doing so, you avoid wasting time and becoming bogged down in the details of talent management planning. In addition, working through these questions will help you to develop a broader, more complete picture of the talent management issues you face as a CTO or executive sponsor of talent management. Specifically, taking the time to think through these decisions can help you:

1. Determine where and how you can direct your talent management efforts to obtain the best results for your organization.

2. Identify the trade-offs that are associated with selecting one strategy over another.

3. Learn how to use these decisions to construct a clearly-articulated leadership talent strategy.

4. Develop a succinct and compelling overview of your game plan for review with your senior executive team and CEO.

With that said, in the next chapter we will take a look at the first of these talent decisions.

Note

1. Malcolm Gladwell, *Blink: The Power of Thinking Without Thinking* (New York: Little, Brown and Company, 2005), pp. 128-136.

CHAPTER 5

STARTING OUT

The Talent Focus Decision

> The most dangerous strategy is to
> jump a chasm in two leaps.
>
> —BENJAMIN DISRAELI

The Talent Focus Decision, otherwise known as the Make/Buy decision, deals with the question of whether you should rely primarily on the use of internal development (Make) or external replacement (Buy) to strengthen your leadership bench. This decision is summarized in Figure 5-1. As I'll discuss at length in this chapter, while all organizations make some use of both approaches, the attempt to straddle these strategies and do "some of both" is likely to simply diffuse your resources and send confusing messages to your organization about what you are attempting to accomplish with your talent development efforts.

At the same time, it's important to keep in mind that, as with the other four talent decisions that I'll be discussing, the Talent Focus Decision isn't irreversible. Over time you may encounter changing business conditions that require you to adapt your talent strategy to shifting requirements. Later in this chapter, I'll provide a few examples of conditions that can prompt such changes to strategy.

Figure 5-1. The Talent Focus Decision.

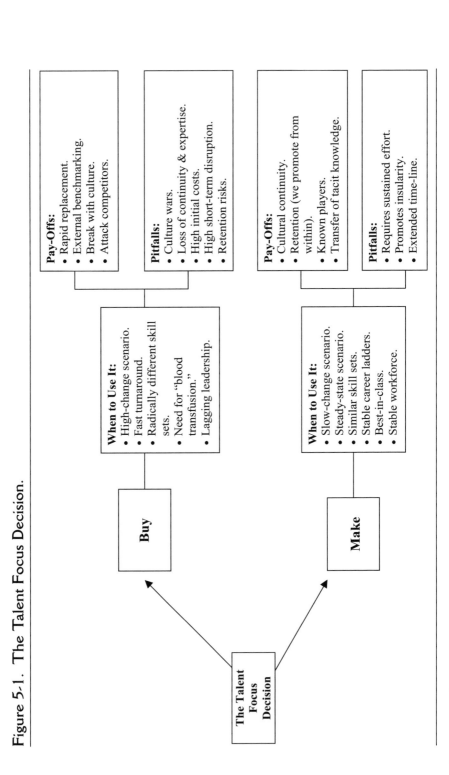

The Make Strategy

Employ the Make Strategy if you assume that business conditions are stable enough to ensure that your leadership career ladders will be relatively stable over the next few years, and that the development experiences you are offering to managers will be applicable to tomorrow's business changes. After all, there is no point in spending the next several years running leaders through formal leadership development training programs, job rotation programs, or mentor programs if the skills that they are developing will be obsolete by the time that they complete such activities.

This decision also assumes that your current internal pool of leadership talent is sufficiently broad and strong. One way to gauge this is to ask yourself how the leaders in your company would fare if they were forced to compete against external job applicants for their own jobs.

Pay-Offs Associated with the Make Strategy

Because the Make Strategy can provide a relatively broad and stable pipeline of leadership talent, it offers a number of advantages. By making use of such development avenues as mentors, cross-functional assignments, job rotations, and formal development programs, it supports organizational continuity by allowing junior-level managers to learn the business from more senior-level executives. Therefore, when compared against the Buy Strategy, this option usually produces leaders who are more knowledgeable about the intricacies of their businesses. A recent study of 373 companies by Hewitt Associates found that the top twenty companies, like GE and Johnson & Johnson, which were characterized by stronger leadership programs, also tended to perform better.[1]

A second advantage of the Make Strategy is that it fosters the continuation of corporate values by filling leadership roles with managers who have been repeatedly tested against those values, and who have been mentored by senior-level executives who model those values. A related advantage is that this strategy supports the transfer of organizational history. By this I mean those thousands of subtle "lessons learned" that senior leaders have gained from years of experience. For managers who work for military contractors, such as Lockheed or Pratt & Whitney, this might involve learning the subtleties of functioning as good business partners to the most important military customers. For a nonprofit organization, these lessons learned might involve learning how to build strong "trust accounts" with influential funding organizations and community stakeholders.

Another advantage involves the nature of managerial on-the-job learning. Much of what managers learn on the job is not anything that can be neatly summarized in a policy statement or procedural manual, but rather consists of that vast body of *tacit knowledge* that managers learn through close-quarter observation and personal experimentation. Tacit knowledge consists of that know-how that is sometimes difficult for managers to articulate and express.[2] At the same time, tacit knowledge has been shown to play a vital role in what has been termed "practical intelligence," the ability to make effective decisions in real-life situations that require anticipating emerging problems, working with problems that are "fuzzy" or ill-formulated, and balancing trade-offs among alternative solutions.[3] From the perspective of talent management, it's important to note that a leader's ability to display tacit knowledge and practical intelligence has been shown to be a strong predictor of leadership success.[4]

A final advantage of the Make Strategy relates to the symbolic meaning that is conveyed with the use of this strategy. When you rely primarily on internal development to build your bench, you send a strong message to your organization that long-term commitment and performance will be recognized and rewarded. This can prove to be an important factor in leadership retention, and can be a very attractive part of your employment-branding proposition to outside job candidates.

Pitfalls Associated with the Make Strategy

A strategy's weaknesses are often a mirror-reflection of its strengths, and the Make Strategy is no exception. First, if you are just launching your internal development, assessment, and succession efforts, be willing to accept the fact that that you are in for a multiyear commitment that will take a few years to begin to show returns. This is particularly likely to be the case when you are identifying and developing mid-level managers to take on executive positions in your company.

A related issue is that the need for such a sustained effort means that your CEO must be willing to keep internal development and selection at the top of the corporate agenda for several years. When a company turns its development efforts off and on again to accommodate each fluctuation in its profit picture, the Make Strategy loses much of its credibility and effectiveness. Sustainability also goes beyond a willingness to invest resources in development. It also means integrating leadership development into business strategy and processes. In the Hewitt study mentioned earlier, top performing companies achieved this integration by taking such steps as linking performance on key leadership competencies to executive compensation, holding leaders accountable for the development of their teams, and using succession planning data to drive promotion and placement decisions for senior managers.[5]

Another drawback that you need to consider is that, over time, companies that become heavily reliant on the Make Strategy can fall into the trap of becoming excessively insular. When this happens, they tend to gauge the strength of their leadership talent solely by historical standards. Thus, they ask themselves the question of whether their managers are getting stronger over time, rather than raise the more fundamental, market-driven question, "How would our managers compare if we forced them to compete for their own jobs against the best external candidates available?" This kind of internal fixation can cause a company to suddenly wake up to find itself woefully behind in the talent curve—simply because it failed to periodically compare its performers against those of outside players.

Finally, there is a paradox at work here, in that companies that create exceptional internal development pipelines eventually run the risk of exposing themselves to raiding parties from other organizations. The reason why corporations such as PepsiCo and GE have traditionally proven to be good hunting grounds for executive recruiters is because recruiters know that these companies have established a strong track record in turning out capable leaders. To combat this problem, you'll need to ensure that your organization's compensation and reward structure is competitive with other organizations in your industry.

The Buy Strategy

Referring back to Figure 5-1, we can see that the Buy Strategy is often employed whenever an organization seeks to jump-start its performance, such as in the case of attempting a quick financial turnaround, or making a leap into a new market. To be successful, these types of corporate mutations may require the whole-scale importing of leaders who are either much stronger than current incumbents, or who bring with them very different backgrounds and skill sets.

This strategy may also prove inevitable when your company is growing so fast that your internal pipeline can't keep with up with your growth projections. In this case, external acquisition may serve as a necessary pump-priming mechanism for accelerating growth. Once you've reached a growth plateau you can always convert to a Make Strategy, as a means of supporting the continued development of those leaders that you've brought on board.

Finally, you may determine that changing business conditions warrant the need for leaders who have completely different skill sets or mind-sets that will simply take too long to develop. This scenario frequently occurs when a new CEO or senior-level executive is brought on board who holds very different views regarding his company's desired direction. In this case, one of the biggest challenges you face is making a quick determination on whether incumbent managers will be able to climb the new performance ramp and take your company to the next level.

At issue here is the fact that not all leadership characteristics are equally developable. Figure 5-2 provides a simplified breakdown of four different categories of leadership characteristics, and the degree to which each set of characteristics can be said to be open to development. At the lowest level are those generic behavioral skills, such as presentation skills or project management skills, that are easily transferable across organizational functions. One step up are those complex skills that require the development of underlying technical competencies or specialized knowledge.

Moving another step up the ladder, I would argue that for those managers who have spent years working within a certain organizational culture, it is even more difficult to make the adaptation to a new cultural environment. While adopting a new cultural mind-set doesn't require a huge intellectual leap, it does involve taking an honest look at deeply ingrained assumptions about such things as what constitutes a high-performing culture, or a high-potential leader. Thus, a leader who has worked for ten years in an entitlement culture will find it very difficult to make the shift to an organization that emphasizes personal accountability and commitment.

At the top of the ladder I place fundamental cognitive factors, such as raw intellectual power. Please don't misunderstand me here. I'm a firm believer that throughout our lives we are able to continue to improve our critical thinking skills by presenting ourselves with new and challenging learning situations. Having said that, however, the fact is that executive-level positions require the ability to deal with complex business situations by quickly sorting through a confusing array of detailed and often incomplete or

Figure 5-2. Determining the degree to which leadership characteristics can be developed.

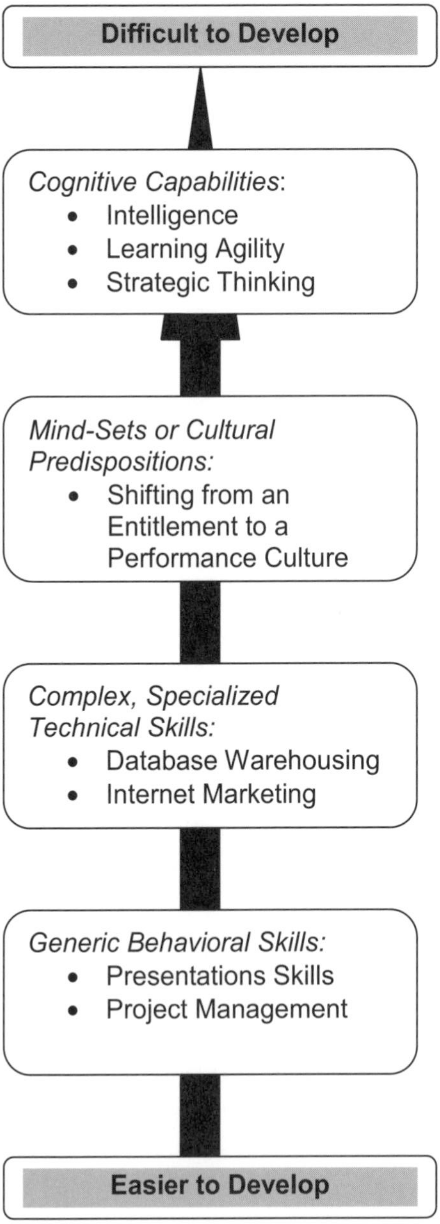

Difficult to Develop

Cognitive Capabilities:
- Intelligence
- Learning Agility
- Strategic Thinking

Mind-Sets or Cultural Predispositions:
- Shifting from an Entitlement to a Performance Culture

Complex, Specialized Technical Skills:
- Database Warehousing
- Internet Marketing

Generic Behavioral Skills:
- Presentations Skills
- Project Management

Easier to Develop

faulty information. In most cases, organizations don't have the luxury of taking their leaders through extended apprenticeships in critical thinking and problem analysis—and the development such programs can provide will never be sufficient to raise a slow learner to the top of the charts. In addition, a number of research studies suggest that as one climbs the executive ladder, raw IQ becomes a more decisive factor in being able to keep up with increased job scope and complexity.[6, 7]

Pay-Offs Associated with the Buy Strategy

The strongest advantage associated with this strategy is that it allows you to undertake the rapid replacement of personnel, particularly when you need to fill senior-level leadership positions and your internal development efforts have just taken root. It can also provide you with opportunities to significantly upgrade your leadership bench, by swapping out those bottom-feeders who comprise the lowest 5 to 10 percent of your leadership talent pool (see the Trade-Up Strategy that is presented in Chapter 7) with stronger performers.

The Buy Strategy can be particularly useful when an organization has been suffering from excessive insularity and "in-breeding." Here's a useful analogy. A fishing merchant was once having a difficult time keeping his catch alive until he reached port. The problem was that the fish he netted simply weren't moving around enough in their holding tank to get sufficient oxygen. His problem was eventually solved when someone suggested putting a predator in the tank with the fish. The moral of the story is that sometimes the introduction of a "predator"—in this case, strong external job candidates—can force complacent managers to "swim faster" and step out of their comfort zones.

A final consideration concerns corporate culture. Just as the Make Strategy is typically used to ensure cultural continuity, the Buy Strategy is often employed to force extensive culture change by searching outside one's organization for candidates who represent a distinct departure from the current culture. By importing managers who share certain key competencies or values, such as a high level of innovation, or the ability to take a strong customer-focused approach to product development, companies can send strong messages to their managers about the types of leadership behavior on which they are placing a premium.

One final advantage of the Buy Strategy is that it can help you build your internal bench strength while simultaneously hamstringing your competitors. In the example that I've just reviewed, as a means of beefing up the company's marketing department the CEO and his senior team conducted extensive raids on the marketing department of one of his strongest competitors. As a result, during the next year the company was able to aggressively eat away at its competitor's market share, leaving the competitor unable to mount an effective counterstroke.

CASE IN POINT: THE MAKE/BUY DECISION

A few years ago I worked for a company that had, over the past forty years, built up a strong entitlement culture. A common belief held by managers in this company was that marginal performance was tolerated, and that only a serious screw-up could cost someone his job. Promotions were made less on demonstrated ability than on the basis of seniority, company loyalty, and the ability to suck up to upper management. Because managers received essentially the same annual increases, over time these increases had come to be viewed as one of many things that the company "owed" to its employees.

When a new CEO was brought on board to undertake a strong performance transition the first step that he took was to replace several members of his executive team. These replacements, in turn, began to search outside the company for stellar performers who had cut their teeth in true high-performance work cultures. This new management team also put in place a strong performance-related incentive program. This change, among other actions implemented by the new team, helped the company achieve a strong turnaround in its performance.

Pitfalls Associated with the Buy Strategy

Unfortunately, the Buy Strategy can prove incredibly costly, since the current market value for top-notch leaders may be quite high when compared to the compensation currently being paid to those incumbents who have slowly worked their way up the internal salary escalator. Add to this the costs associated with severance packages for displaced managers, relocation, and executive recruiting expenses for outside candidates, and the bill quickly rises.

The Buy Strategy can also prove to be very disruptive to an organization if it takes the form of the rapid, large-scale importing of outside talent. If you find yourself in this scenario, you will need to create a transition plan that can help you keep your organizational units in motion during the six- to twelve-month period in which acquisition and on-boarding is underway. Another caution is that excessive reliance on this strategy can create a retention risk for those leaders who, fearing for their own job security, may preemptively jump ship and leave your company.

Still another drawback associated with the use of the Buy Strategy is that, when compared with the Make Strategy, it typically requires organizations to accept a higher level of risk for their leadership staffing decisions. The reason for this is that rather than promoting leaders who have been repeatedly tested against tough business challenges, under this strategy you are hiring managers who are relatively unknown to your organization. At issue here is the question of whether these outsiders will be able to successfully "graft on" to your organization. By this I mean not only whether outside candidates have the technical and leadership skills needed to successfully perform in their jobs, but also whether they represent a good culture-fit to your organization.

Studies performed by the Center for Creative Leadership and Right Associates show that about 35 percent of new managers and executives fail within their first eighteen months on the job.[8,9] The top reasons given for these failures are the inability to form strong relationships with peers, stakeholders, and subordinates; failure to achieve their objectives; and lack of political acumen.

Matching Leadership Competencies to Business Requirements

The Make and Buy strategies are based on developing or hiring leaders who have the skills and experience needed to help their organizations succeed. This leads us to the obvious question of whether there exists a generic, "one-size-fits-all" template for the ideal competencies that executives and managers should have, or whether these leadership profiles vary as a function of business requirements. There is evidence to suggest that the latter is the case, and that before attempting to develop or hire leaders we need to consider how leadership needs vary in relation to the strategic needs of an organization. Two research studies provide support for this.

The first, dealing with CEO succession, was initiated several years ago by the National Association of Corporate Directors (NACD) through a Blue Ribbon Commission on CEO succession.[10] Data gathered from seven senior-level HR leaders, each of which with extensive experience in executive succession, was compiled to identify those CEO behaviors which are critically important to success in the four different business scenarios characterized by 1) managing rapid growth, 2) managing a business turnaround, 3) dealing with a merger integration, and 4) leading a company through an industry shift. As is shown in Figure 5-3, the HR leaders who participated in this study believe that leadership competencies for CEOs vary strongly by the type of business challenge that a company is facing.

The second piece of research was conducted by ISR LLC, a Chicago-based, global employee research and consulting firm. ISR examined the financial performance of thirty-one companies, and also conducted surveys with over 9,000 employees from a variety

Figure 5-3. The relationship between organizational requirements and key leadership factors.

Corporate Situation	Key Leadership Factors
Rapid Growth	• Sees alternatives beyond traditions and habits. • Embraces change easily. • Effectively communicates clear vision of the future. • Is willing to surround self with needed talent. • Delegates authority; trusts others to get the job done.
Turnaround	• Has near-term focus with long-term awareness. • Stands ground in face of resistance. • Is clear and concise communicator. • Motivates people to think about where the company is going—not where it is coming from. • Generates a solid team around a new agenda.
Merger Integration	• Is able to visualize picture of future organization. • Understands the cultures of the two organizations and potential implications of their differences. • Recognizes that cultures are more powerful than individuals; willing to work with cultural dynamics. • Uses consensus-building management style.
Industry Shift	• Has excellent industry knowledge. • Is able to think out of the box. • Is comfortable with ambiguity. • Has passion for change. • Creates a sense of urgency. • Motivates others to change their mind-sets as well as their management practices.

of companies spanning ten nations. As is illustrated in Figure 5-4, the results of the survey suggest that organizations that are facing very different business challenges place very different values on certain leadership competencies.

Specifically:

- Companies that focus on *developing a strong brand and image* place great importance on the leadership skills related to

Figure 5-4. Distinguishing leadership themes by strategic priority. Extracted with permission from *A Contingent Approach to Leadership Effectiveness* by Patrick Kulesa, Global Research Director, ISR LLC. 2005.

communicating the importance of that brand to their employees. Leaders in these companies must excel in such areas as providing clear goals and direction, dealing effectively with change, and providing a clear vision for the future.

• Companies that focus on *customer service* must be able to communicate the importance of customer service through communicating a congruent set of company values, and by setting clear standards, performance expectations, and consequences for meeting customer service values. Accordingly, these leaders have to model high integrity and know how to empower employees to deliver quality service.

• Companies that focus on *efficiency* succeed on the basis of speed and the ability to develop cost-effective methods for moving their goods into their markets. Such companies emphasize the leadership skills of efficiently executing on tasks and projects by effectively managing time-lines and resources. Such companies must also be adept at soliciting, and acting upon, employees' ideas.

• Finally, companies that focus on *innovation* provide a "clear line of sight" for employees by keeping employees informed and aligned on organizational goals, priorities, and changes, and through the quick implementation of ideas and decisions.[11]

When viewed together, these research studies emphasize the importance of clearly thinking through, and articulating the connection between, an organization's strategic priorities and the kinds of leadership skills and competencies that are needed to drive those priorities.

Notes

1. *Research Highlights: How the Top 20 Companies Grow Great Leaders*, Hewitt Associates, LLC., 2005.

2. Robert J. Sternberg et al., *Practical Intelligence in Everyday Life* (New York: Cambridge University Press, 2000).

3. Richard K. Wagner and Robert J. Sternberg, "Tacit Knowledge in Managerial Success," *Journal of Business and Psychology* 1, 4 (1987): 301–312.

4. Robert J. Sternberg and Jennifer Hedlund, "Practical Intelligence, g, and Work Psychology," *Human Performance* 15, 1&2 (2002): 143–160.

5. *Research Highlights: How the Top 20 Companies Grow Great Leaders.*

6. Frank L. Schmidt and John Hunter, "General Mental Ability in the World of Work: Occupational Attainment and Work Performance," *Journal of Personality and Social Psychology* 86, 1 (2004): 162–173.

7. "The Validity and Utility of Selection Methods in Personnel Psychology: Practical and Theoretical Implications of 85 Years of Research Findings," *Psychological Bulletin* 124, 2 (1998): 263–274.

8. Press Release; Right Associates, March 8, 2005. www.corporate-ir.net/ireye/ir_site.zhtml?ticker = rht&script = 410&layout = 0& item_id = 682974.

9. S. H. Davis, "Executive Gain," *Accountancy Age*, March 18, 2005.

10. This information was extracted from Robert Barner, *Executive Resource Management* (Palo Alto, Calif: Davies-Black, 2000): 299–301.

11. This information was extracted from the research report, *A Contingent Approach to Leadership Effectiveness*, by Patrick Kulesa, Global Research Director, ISR LLC, 2005.

CHAPTER 6

TALENT
DEVELOPMENT DECISIONS

And so one skilled at employing the military

Takes them by the hand as if leading a single

person.

They cannot hold back.

—SUN TZU, *THE ART OF WAR*

This chapter introduces two key decisions related to leadership talent development. The Capstone/Foundation Decision, which is summarized in Figure 6-1, considers those organizational conditions under which it is more effective to either concentrate or disperse your talent development efforts. The Stream/Pool Decision, shown in Figure 6-2, provides two very different approaches to the challenge of identifying and developing candidates for leadership succession and placement. Together, these two decisions provide a useful framework for growing a strong leadership bench.

The Capstone/Foundation Decision

Let's assume that you've made the decision to pursue a Make Strategy and build your talent base largely through internal development. Given this decision, you then need to decide whether to achieve this development by focusing the bulk your company's time and resources on identified high-potential leaders (Capstone Strategy), or whether you are better off dispersing these resources across the broader base of your leadership bench (Foundation Strategy). The respective advantages and disadvantages associated with the use of each strategy are outlined in Figure 6-1. Let's consider each of these options and see what they yield in terms of pay-offs and pitfalls.

The Foundation Strategy

You might wish to pursue the Foundation Strategy when you are working within a relative small company or division, one that has no more than a few hundred managers. In this case, it becomes feasible to spread your development efforts across your leadership ranks, take the time to work closely with your executive team to assess each manager's suitability for promotion, and craft individual development plans for each manager.

An organization may also decide to pursue this strategy when it is attempting to employ its leadership development efforts as part of a culture-change process, by helping to get managers aligned around a common set of values and corporate strategy. The idea here is to have senior-level executives take the lead in guiding those efforts, and by so doing make strong statements about the kinds of leadership behaviors that they model and endorse.

Pay-Offs Associated with the Foundation Strategy

Going back to the concept of symbolic messages, in choosing the Foundation Strategy you send a strong message that your organization views its leaders as having equal potential and worth. This message is very congruent with corporate cultures such as that found in Southwest Airlines, which places a lot of emphasis on

Figure 6-1. The Capstone or Foundation Decision.

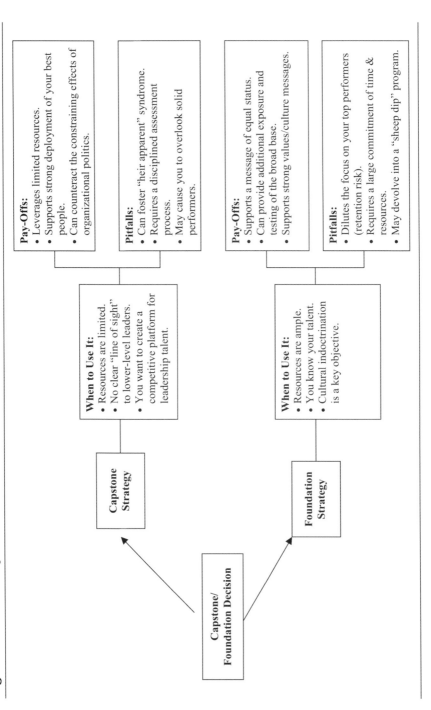

Pay-Offs:
- Leverages limited resources.
- Supports strong deployment of your best people.
- Can counteract the constraining effects of organizational politics.

Pitfalls:
- Can foster "heir apparent" syndrome.
- Requires a disciplined assessment process.
- May cause you to overlook solid performers.

When to Use It:
- Resources are limited.
- No clear "line of sight" to lower-level leaders.
- You want to create a competitive platform for leadership talent.

Capstone Strategy

Pay-Offs:
- Supports a message of equal status.
- Can provide additional exposure and testing of the broad base.
- Supports strong values/culture messages.

Pitfalls:
- Dilutes the focus on your top performers (retention risk).
- Requires a large commitment of time & resources.
- May devolve into a "sheep dip" program.

When to Use It:
- Resources are ample.
- You know your talent.
- Cultural indoctrination is a key objective.

Foundation Strategy

Capstone/ Foundation Decision

esprit de corps and teamwork as core corporate values. For these reasons, the Foundation Strategy can be a strong motivational tool for building solid performers.

Another argument for this approach is that by insuring that all managers have at least a minimal level of development support, this strategy helps to establish a baseline level of competence across the organization.

If conducted effectively, large-scale leadership programs can also be used to assess leadership potential for advancement. This can be accomplished by running large numbers of managers through 360° reviews or management simulations that provide managers with feedback on their leadership competencies. Another approach involves the use of *action learning programs,* in which managers are formed into part-time teams to tackle important business problems. After working together for several weeks these teams are then asked to report back on their findings to panels of senior executives. The reporting-out process provides senior managers with an excellent vehicle for evaluating such leadership competencies as strategic thinking, problem solving, communication skills, and business savvy.

The types of broad-based development programs that are typically incorporated into the Foundation Strategy can also be used to provide senior managers with a common platform for presenting critical messages about organizational values, strategy, and performance standards. A related application is to use these programs as a platform for making a compelling case for business change.

Pitfalls Associated with the Foundation Strategy

As you can see from Figure 6-1, one drawback of the Foundation Strategy is that it requires a large commitment in time and resources to support a broad and sustained management development effort. These efforts frequently take the form of formal leadership development training programs that are mandatory for all managers, and which are customized to meet the different needs of each leadership level. Such a heavy resource investment is often difficult to maintain. I've witnessed many companies that have launched large leadership development programs with great fanfare, only to see them collapse after a few years. Once the momentum is gone its hard to reestablish such programs because by then, your managers have been receiving mixed messages about the relative importance of leadership development.

Unfortunately, such a broad-based investment can dilute your focus on your best performers, leaving you with little time and energy for the kinds of resource-intensive programs (such as advanced management programs at Ivy League colleges, job rotation programs, or high-potential development programs) that are geared toward a company's star performers. As a result, these super-performers could become frustrated and leave your organization for competitors who can lure them with the promise of unique development options and incentive programs. Your challenge, then, is to look for ways to provide leadership development support to all managers, while finding ways, such as incentive-based compensation programs, to recognize the efforts of your top performers.

For a large organization comprised of several divisions or strategic business units (SBUs), another problem involves developing a structured vehicle for obtaining a clear "line of sight" to managers deeper into the organization. A company that has several thousand managers dispersed across different organizational units, time zones, and countries will probably find it difficult to identify and keep track of all of its leaders. While some organizations rely on the heads of their business units to keep their senior executives apprised of their best talent, there are three reasons why this tactic may prove insufficient:

1. It is highly unlikely that all executives employ the same leadership standards or qualifying criteria for selecting high-

potential performers. As a result, you may find yourself attempting to make tough talent calls based on an "apples-to-oranges" assessment of talent.

2. Some managers will inevitably hoard their best talent and keep them hidden from view, or may feel that their commitment to managing leadership talent ends at the boundaries of their organizational units. As a result, they may lack the time, knowledge, or interest needed to inquire into career pathways or developmental opportunities for managers that extend outside the boundaries of their organizations.

3. Each divisional manager tends to assess "leadership potential" in terms of the relatively restrictive domain defined by his or her own business function. This is a bit like a high school coach contending that the track stars in his small rural school are the best in the nation based only on knowledge of competitors in his immediate school district. A very different scenario occurs when you are working with a corporate-managed talent base that allows you to calibrate leadership potential on an enterprise-wide scope. I've taken part in many leadership talent reviews within five different companies, and the one thing that never fails to amaze me is how widely skewed assessments of high-potential leadership can be when senior executives are left to construct their own unique standards for "leadership potential."

The very size of the programs encompassed in this strategy makes it difficult to maintain quality standards. Large-scale leadership development programs can easily degenerate into "sheep-dip" programs, in which the emphasis switches from meeting the unique development needs of each manager to giving all managers a cursory "dip" in the same, watered-down development experience.

The Capstone Strategy

Whereas the Foundation Strategy disperses talent management efforts across a company's entire leadership talent base, the Capstone Strategy focuses the bulk of development support on those leaders who have been identified as having the highest potential to advance and take on broader responsibilities in an organization. This strategy rests on three underlying beliefs:

1. You believe that within your organization there are a few managers who demonstrate a significantly higher degree of potential for long-term advancement, when compared against their internal counterparts.

2. It is possible to accurately identify these leaders within your overall organization.

3. You believe that once these individuals are identified and developed, they should be able to perform well within a wide variety of organizational settings.

Given these assumptions, identified high-potential managers are usually assumed to constitute an exemplary group that can be leveraged across a variety of organizational challenges. A quick look at Figure 6-1 shows that there are three business conditions that warrant the use of this strategy:

• The Capstone Strategy is frequently employed when an organization wants to focus its limited resources on providing an intensive, high-impact, development, assessment, and retention process for its strongest performers.

• This approach is also typically seen in large, dispersed organizations, where it is hard to obtain a clear "line of sight" on lower-level managers. By identifying high-potential performers early in their career and carefully tracking their progress, executives ensure that these star performers don't disappear from their view.

• Finally, the Capstone Strategy is sometimes introduced as part of a broader business objective to induce competitiveness into a complacent leadership structure. By launching a program that seeks to identify, recognize, and reward top-notch talent, your

CEO and executive team send a strong symbolic message that your organization is moving toward a high-performance culture, and that your managers are now operating in a highly competitive arena. For that reason, the creation of a high-potential development program can also serve as a strong recruiting mechanism for world-class talent—the kinds of leaders who welcome rigorous competition.

Pay-Offs Associated with the Capstone Strategy
Perhaps the strongest advantage associated with this strategy is that it helps you keep your best people in your line of sight, wherever they happen to move in your organization. Having a Capstone Strategy in place means that you can quickly determine who is most likely to take full advantage of limited and expensive development opportunities. An example would be selecting one or two leaders to attend the type of multiple-week, university-sponsored Advanced Management Program that can easily cost an organization $20,000 to $50,000 for each participant.

The Capstone Strategy also allows you to leverage organizational performance by allowing you to quickly identify and deploy your strongest talent to meet such tough business challenges as the sudden departure of a star player, or the unanticipated entrance of a new market competitor. This strategy provides a mechanism for the pre-identification of leaders who can be quickly mobilized to tackle such challenges.

Finally, the Capstone Strategy can help you counteract the constraining effects of organizational politics by installing a clear, equitable, and uniform process for talent assessment, development, and deployment. If you are able to construct a company-wide mechanism for identifying and tracking your best performers, it becomes harder for executives to hoard talent. In the same way, organizational assessments of leadership potential are less likely to be biased by relying solely on the views of leaders' immediate managers.

Pitfalls Associated with the Capstone Strategy

While the Capstone Strategy can keep your organization focused on its high-potential leaders, this strategy may also fuel resentment among those strong, but not stellar, performers who fall just short of entry into the high-potential group. To combat this you will need to give some creative attention to the steps you will take to recognize and motivate these mid-range performers.

You also need to consider that while the use of the Capstone Strategy may well reduce your overall cost for leadership development, your per-person cost is likely to go up. This is because the types of development opportunities that are subsumed in this strategy tend to involve such individualized and expensive vehicles as university programs, internal or external coaching or mentoring, assignments to temporary project teams, job rotations, or short- or long-term job assignments. As a result, under this strategy a heavier investment risk is associated with each managerial participant. A mid-level manager could who walks out the door two years after initial hire may represent a wasted investment of $20,000 to $50,000 in corporate development costs.

Another concern with the Capstone Strategy is that it can lead to the "heir apparent" syndrome. In this situation, high-potential managers who have been informed of their status begin to hold inflated assessments of their own worth and unrealistic expectations for future advancement. To prevent this problem, it is important to manage participants' expectations, and encourage participants to engage in realistic self-appraisals of future job opportunities.

The Challenge of Accurately Assessing Leadership Potential

If you are going to focus the bulk of your time, money, and attention on a few identified high-potential players, you'd better have your assessment process in order. This means establishing clear guidelines that executives can follow in measuring leadership performance and potential, providing uniform standards for evaluating these factors, and developing some assessment measures that extend beyond the traditional annual performance review. Organizations that initiate this strategy without first having in place an effective assessment process run the risk of not only making bad judgment calls on leaders, but of allowing their promotion and succession process to degenerate into a political tug-of-war. (Figure 6-2 provides a breakdown of alternative leadership assessment vehicles). A related issue is that it's important to carefully think through the implementation guidelines that your organizational will follow in purchasing, designing, applying, and monitoring leadership assessment instruments. As a starting point for developing your own guidelines, Figure 6-3 provides a series of recommended guidelines for managing the administration of assessment activities.

When attempting to make accurate judgment calls on leadership potential, it is important to be able to identify those key causal factors that influence the development of leadership potential. Some of the best research in this field has been done by the Corporate Leadership Council, which recently completed a major research study on high-potential managers, involving survey data collected from 11,000 employees from 59 organizations and 29 countries.[1] This study was unique in that, rather than simply ask respondents to rate the perceived value of different causal factors, the research team identified those senior executives who were named by their companies as being in the top quartile of their management populations. In doing so, they created "top performer profiles," showing how these senior executives rated (through both self-ratings and ratings by their direct managers) on three dimensions of leadership potential:

• *Ability*–both intellectual ability and technical/functional and interpersonal skills. This factor was measured through a rating scale completed by employees' managers.

Figure 6-2. Alternative vehicles for assessing leadership potential.

Assessment Vehicles	Descriptions
Performance Appraisals	• **Defined:** Yearly evaluations as assessed against performance on objectives and selected leadership competencies. • **Advantages:** Easy to implement, provides detailed information on performance. • **Shortfalls:** Feedback is restricted to immediate manager (rater bias) and doesn't assess future potential.
Team Interviews	• **Defined:** Joint interviews by 3–5 senior executives to assess leadership potential through use of a uniform rating system. • **Advantages:** Provides feedback and buy-in from multiple senior stakeholders and forces alignment on assessment standards and criteria. • **Shortfalls:** Provides a distinct advantage to those managers who excel in interviewing, while not fully assessing long-term performance record.
360° Reviews	• **Defined:** Multi-rater feedback from peers, direct reports, and one's manager, typically compared against internal or external populations. • **Advantages:** Provides anonymous feedback from a variety of stakeholder groups, and often provides information on leadership style factors related to success or derailment. • **Shortfalls:** Assesses leadership style within current position; doesn't include data on performance results, nor does it provide an accurate assessment of potential for further advancement.
Intelligence Testing	• **Defined:** Standard IQ tests, such as the Watson-Glaser or the Ravens Progressive Matrices, which assess both the ability to make reasoned judgments and ability to work with abstract concepts. • **Advantages:** Provides a clear scorecard on critical thinking skills, with comparisons against broad-based executive and professional norms.

(continues)

Figure 6-2. Continued.

Assessment Vehicles	Descriptions
Intelligence Testing	• **Shortfalls:** Research suggests that IQ is typically more important as a success factor for senior-level executive positions than for mid-level positions. Doesn't assess other related factors such as EQ (emotional intelligence) or tacit knowledge and "practical intelligence." Also, requires stringent testing process by a qualified I/O psychologist. May need to include nonverbal assessments, such as the Ravens Progressive Matrices, to eliminate culture or language biases.
Personality Assessment	• **Defined:** Written assessments that are aimed at profiling the leader's personality. • **Advantages:** Provides a simple way of encapsulating the personality and leadership style of managers. • **Shortfalls:** Buyer beware; many assessment instruments lack validity and are employed by individuals who lack a Ph.D. in psychology. Many of these assessments provide only global assessments of personality, and little data in the way of specifics regarding leadership style.
Learning Agility Assessment	• **Defined:** Multi-rater feedback that is aimed at assessing a leader's adaptability and ability to learn in new and challenging situations. • **Advantages:** One of the few vehicles that provides multiple views of a manager's ability to learn on the job, which is one of the strongest predictors of potential for advancement. • **Shortfalls:** Requires feedback providers who are close enough to the leader to make this type of assessment. Also, validity varies by instrument. Two recommended instruments are e-Choices (Lominger, Inc.) and Profiler (Center for Creative Leadership).
Assessment Against Competency Models	• **Defined:** An assessment by one's manager or others against a series of defined leadership competencies. Typically used in conjunction with 360° instruments. • **Advantages:** Provides managers with a common language and yardstick for assessing leadership talent.

	• **Shortfalls:** Can prove to be bulky and more of a paper-drill if the list of competencies is extensive, too abstract, and lacks behavioral examples.
Multi-Level Assessment	• **Defined:** Involves successive, comparative reviews of leaders by different levels of management on the same rating dimensions. • **Advantages:** Supports a recalibration of talent ratings at each successive level, and forces intense dialogues between managers and their bosses on leadership standards and performance expectations. • **Shortfalls:** Requires a clear set of scorecards and guidelines in order for the discussions to be driven by objective measures. Also requires senior executives to have exposure to the performance of lower-level managers.
Assessment Centers	• **Defined:** Candidates are observed and rated on leadership competencies as they perform on a series of structured management simulations. • **Advantages:** Enables you to compare leader performance within the same series of situations, thus providing an even playing field. The use of outside observers/raters removes politics from the assessment. • **Shortfalls:** Can be extremely expensive and time-intensive, usually from $3,000 to $10,000 per candidate, and one to three days of candidate time.

• *Engagement*—the degree of discretionary effort and personal commitment to the job. This was measured by having employees complete a self-report measure on the survey.

• *Aspiration*—the degree to which employees seek out greater responsibility, advancement, etc. This factor was measured by having employees complete a self-report measure on the survey.

The next step involved correlating these three measures with the probability of being a top performer at the senior level. This allowed the research group to establish a weighting for each dimension, based on how much or how little it distinguished top perform-

Figure 6-3. Guidelines for assessment administration.

Leader Assessment Guidelines

1. Use only well-established techniques that have been developed by qualified vendors. Be wary of consultants who peddle their own home-grown leadership assessment tools, since if you use an assessment approach that hasn't been sufficiently tested and validated you open your organization up to poor talent calls. Beyond this, you may expose your organization to potential liability for making leadership evaluations based on unproven methods. To avoid this problem, I recommend that when using psychological assessments you work through a Industrial-Organizational (I/O) or Clinical Psychologist who has a Ph.D. from a reputable school, and a state license to practice in either of these areas.

2. If you are unsure about the validity and reliability of a psychological assessment instrument, look it up in a standard reference guide such as the *Mental Measurements Yearbook*.

3. Before you begin down this path, create a written policy detailing how your assessment instruments will be used, the HR leader who will be responsible for directing or managing these activities, and who will have to assess the final assessment reports. My personal recommendation here is that all written assessment documentation on organizational leaders should be retained by, and managed by, a single HR leader.

4. A key decision you need to make at this point is what and how assessment feedback will be shared with assessed leaders. I recommend that assessed leaders be provided with written summaries of 360° feedback, and with only verbal summaries that highlight the developmental aspects of any psychological assessments that have been employed.

5. Clearly explain to your leaders whether assessment data will be used for development, or selection and promotion decisions.

6. When using a 360° tool, don't overwhelm raters with hundreds of items and dozens of leadership competencies. Include no more than a dozen leadership competencies. For each competency, provide a clear definition and a list of behavioral anchors that provide examples of how demonstrated proficiency in that competency would be initiated. If you are developing your own 360° tool, use a consultant who has demonstrated solid experience in this area. Generic, well-validated leadership competency models are available from Lominger, Inc. and the Center for Creative Leadership.

7. When using any assessment instrument, check to see if the consulting firm you are using has obtained aggregate data and benchmark norms from thousands of other employees in different companies. Ask for a report that summarizes these norms. They should provide you with a means of calibrating your leaders' test scores against a broader base of managers.

8. Be careful of assuming that assessment instruments that have been designed and normed in the United States will work equally well in other countries. Certain assessment instruments may be culturally-biased, or the data gathering approach that they employ may not work well in another culture.

9. Use multiple approaches to establish a system of checks and balances on your assessment conclusions.

10. Make certain that before you proceed with an assessment approach, it has been reviewed with, and approved by, your CEO and senior executive team.

ers at the senior level. The study's researchers then asked leaders one management level lower in the organization to complete the same "top performance" profiles, and compared their results with those found for top-quartile executives. Following this process, those mid-level leaders who were found to have at least a 75 percent chance of being a top performer at the next level were designated as being high potential leaders.

Among the useful findings from the Corporate Leadership Council (CLC) study was the fact that only 29 percent of all high-performing managers were identified as being true high-potential leaders.[2] Furthermore, the study showed that the factors of aspiration, ability, and engagement take on different importance as one ascends the management ladder. While all three factors weighed out as being equally important for junior-level managers, ability and engagement were almost equally important for assessing the potential of mid-level managers, with aspiration being far less important. For senior-level managers, ability was the most important factor, followed by engagement, with aspiration being almost a negligible factor.[3]

In addition, this study points to the emergence of three distinct development profiles for those managers who were not identified as being high-potential leaders. For each of these profiles, researchers calculated the likelihood that managers would be successful at the next management level, based on the degree to which their profiles matched the overall success profiles found for "top performance" senior managers.[4]

- Ten percent of these managers, the "engaged dreamers," scored high on the factors of aspiration and engagement, but low on ability. The study calculated that these managers had no chance for success at the next management level.

- Forty-three percent of these managers, the "unengaged stars," scored relative high on the factors of aspiration and ability, but low on engagement. The study found that these managers had a 13 percent chance of success at the next management level.

•   Forty-seven percent of these managers, the "misaligned stars," scored relatively high on ability and engagement, but low on aspiration. In other words, "they simply didn't 'want it' enough."[5] The study found that these managers had a 44 percent chance of success at the next management level. Of all three groups, this was the group that stood the greatest chance for success, assuming that they could develop the drive for advancement.

This research provides a useful model for framing the concept of "leadership potential" and for examining the relative impact on potential of the factors of ability, aspiration, and engagement.

Suggestions for Effectively Leveraging the Capstone Strategy

If you are going to make use of the Capstone Strategy, make certain that you have access to information on your best performers. Here are three examples from my own past:

•   Have a process for tracking the hiring source for identified high-potential (HIPO) leaders. In doing this with one company we found that a large percentage of our strongest players had been hired through one small boutique executive recruiting firm, while none of the managers that we obtained through a much larger recruiting firm ended up on our HIPO list. As a result of this review we decided to shift a much larger portion of our recruiting efforts over to the smaller firm.

•   In another work setting we interviewed our HIPO leaders and their managers to identify developmental experiences that appeared to provide them with the greatest value. While a number of benchmark studies have provided generic information on the types of development experiences that are important for leadership development (data is available from McKinsey, Inc., The Corporate

Leadership Council, and the Center for Creative Leadership) data from these types of interviews can help you to focus more effectively on your developmental resources.

•   In one company, we conducted an organization-wide employee satisfaction and retention survey, subdivided by site location, management level, and by high-potential status (whether or not respondents had been identified as HIPO leaders). The results were very revealing. One of the strongest issues for employees—company-wide—was the issue of work-life balance, particularly in terms of length of work hours. However this was a minor issue for the HIPO participants, who were much more concerned with obtaining challenging work and obtaining differential rewards (pay raises and bonuses) for meeting results. This data proved very valuable to us as we attempted to move this company from an entitlement culture to a performance culture.

Aligning Talent Strategies with Leadership Incentives

One way to determine whether a company maintains a Capstone or Foundation Strategy is to perform a quick check on their executive compensation system. Companies that foster a Foundation Strategy are more likely to employ some type of "employee sharing" plan that disperses incentive bonuses across the management population in an equitable distribution, as determined by the company's overall performance against selected financial targets. In the same way, stock options are usually doled out according to one's management level, with all managers within a given level being given the same option allotment.

In contrast, companies that employ the Capstone Strategy typically require their leaders to meet minimal performance standards in order to be eligible for the company's bonus and option pools. In addition, within such organizations incentive levels are at least partially determined by each individual's ability to meet or exceed set performance objectives.

Leveraging Resources to Foster Leadership Development

Regardless of whether organizations opt for the Foundation or Capstone Strategy, they all face the challenge of determining how to meet identified leadership development needs with limited resources. As you attempt to tackle this challenge, it is important to note that available research suggests that not all developmental experiences are equally valuable to leaders. A review of this research can prove helpful if you are attempting to leverage limited management development resources across a wide cross-section of organizational leaders.

A research study conducted by McKinsey & Company of 6,000 executives in the top 200 positions in fifty large U.S. companies found a wide variation in the perceived value of leadership development activities.[6] Figure 6-4 provides a summary of part of these research findings.

Note that when respondents were asked to rate various leadership development activities both on relative importance and on their organizations' effectiveness in implementing these activities, traditional classroom training programs came up fairly low on both measures, while the four highest-scoring activities were as follows:

1. The way in which a job is structured (whether it provides sufficient scope, work variety, and responsibility to foster growth)
2. The speed at which individuals move through a series of job assignments to stretch learning
3. The incorporation of challenge into job assignments (such as working in a staff role that requires leaders to manage through influence)

Figure 6-4. The comparative importance of different leadership development activities. (Please note that these activities are classified into three different categories: a) formal training, b) on-the-job training, and c) feedback and monitoring.)

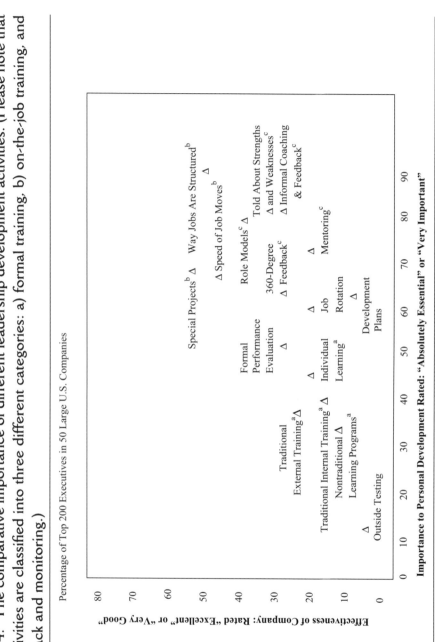

Percentage of Top 200 Executives in 50 Large U.S. Companies

4. The availability of learning through senior-level models and mentors[7]

The study referenced earlier by the Corporate Leadership Council on high-potential managers provides additional support to the idea that management experiences differed widely in their ability to develop leadership potential. The four top-rated management experiences in this study were:

1. Having to make an evaluation on another employee's potential for leadership
2. Leading teams
3. Developing a strategy for a department
4. Evaluating the needs of global employees when developing teams

The next four highest-rated experiences (all of which were rated as having the same contribution value toward developing leadership potential) were:

1. Assessing employee performance
2. Developing work plans to guide reports
3. Assessing project performance
4. Managing projects involving new customers

Other possible development experiences, such as "managing employees with more technical knowledge than you," "managing budgets," or "making difficult decisions to get struggling projects on track" were rated far lower.[8] The three most important personal experiences found to be related to the development of leadership potential were (in order of relative importance): (1) having to "modify work to adapt to changing circumstances," (2) being tasked to "creatively solve problems," and (3) having to "persuade senior managers to take difficult actions."[9]

There are two important takeaways from these two research studies. The first is that on-the-job development experiences tend to be far more relevant and applicable for building leadership competence than are formal training programs. Therefore, if you are going to invest money in any single training activity, consider a program that shows managers how to stage on-the-job development experiences to allow their direct reports to extract the greatest benefit from these experiences. Second, given that not all on-the-job development experiences are equally important to building leadership bench strength, concentrate on those few that are most likely to generate the greatest value for your organization.

The Talent Stream or Talent Pool Decision

The Talent Stream/Pool Decision shapes the nature of your organization's leadership succession process. The Talent Stream Strategy relies on identifying specific successor candidates for targeted leadership positions. By contrast, the Talent Pool Strategy is based on identifying pools of high-potential leaders at selected management levels who can serve as qualified candidates to fill alternative leadership positions as these positions become available. Additional information on these two different strategies is presented in Figure 6-5.

When to Use the Stream Strategy

Consider selecting this strategy when the following conditions exist in your organization:

- You have a limited managerial population, meaning that you have few successor candidates from which to draw upon, and your talent population is too restricted to allow for the creation of a robust pool.

Figure 6-5. The Talent Stream or Pool Decision.

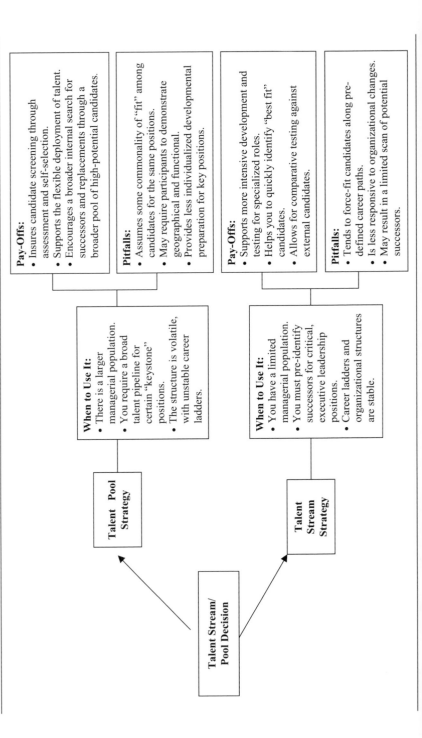

**Talent Stream/
Pool Decision**

**Talent Pool
Strategy**

When to Use It:
- There is a larger managerial population.
- You require a broad talent pipeline for certain "keystone" positions.
- The structure is volatile, with unstable career ladders.

Pay-Offs:
- Insures candidate screening through assessment and self-selection.
- Supports the flexible deployment of talent.
- Encourages a broader internal search for successors and replacements through a broader pool of high-potential candidates.

Pitfalls:
- Assumes some commonality of "fit" among candidates for the same positions.
- May require participants to demonstrate geographical and functional.
- Provides less individualized developmental preparation for key positions.

**Talent
Stream
Strategy**

When to Use It:
- You have a limited managerial population.
- You must pre-identify successors for critical, executive leadership positions.
- Career ladders and organizational structures are stable.

Pay-Offs:
- Supports more intensive development and testing for specialized roles.
- Helps you to quickly identify "best fit" candidates.
- Allows for comparative testing against external candidates.

Pitfalls:
- Tends to force-fit candidates along pre-defined career paths.
- Is less responsive to organizational changes.
- May result in a limited scan of potential successors.

- Career ladders and organizational structures are stable, making it feasible to create three- to five-year development plans for identified successors.
- You are attempting to pre-identify successors for critical, executive leadership positions. This will typically be the case for those leadership positions that:
  - Are at a senior-executive level and exert a major impact on your organization's overall performance
  - Are unique in structure and difficult to fill (in the aftermath of the Sarbanes-Oxley Act, I would argue that vice presidents or senior vice presidents of corporate audit and compliance would fall into this category)
  - Require an extended ramp-up and apprenticeship period to fully prepare leaders for unique job demands that may be largely outside the range of experience of most managers (in other words, positions that require the "custom fitting" of successor candidates)

Two points need to be mentioned here. First, succession planning shouldn't be confused with simple replacement planning, in which the objective is to identify managers who could step in as interim replacements in emergency situations. Instead, it is intended to identify those managers who could, within the next five years, function as strong successors. Given that business conditions can change radically over this time-period, an important part of this task involves anticipating changes in business conditions or organizational structure that could dramatically shift the criteria for successors.

Consider the situation in which you are trying to identify successor candidates for the position of chief human resources officer for your organization. If your five-year business plan calls for making your first move into the international market, the criteria for this position might shift to include experience in international compensation or organizational development, despite the fact that the current incumbent may lack these qualifications.

On a separate note, I am finding that organizations that employ the Stream Strategy are beginning to apply it more selectively. That is, rather than attempt to construct written succession plans for *all* leadership positions, CTOs are finding it more effective to limit succession planning to those few management positions that are considered to be mission-critical to organizational success.

Pay-Offs Associated with the Stream Strategy

Because this strategy focuses on identifying and developing successors for a few key executive positions, it allows you to engage in a more intensive development process for those successor candidates. That is, it enables you to focus additional time and attention on obtaining an in-depth understanding of the current leadership requirements for these positions and to carefully consider how these requirements are likely to change over time. In this way, you can handpick the "best fit" successor candidates for each position.

For the same reasons, given that you are dealing with a very limited population, this strategy allows you to select developmental actions that, because of their intensity and expense, would not normally be made available to successor candidates in high-potential pools. Some examples are:

• Loaning successor candidates out to other company units for three to six months to assist in special projects, such as a facilities build-out, a business turnaround plan, or the launch of a new project.

• Placing successor candidates in intense mentoring relationships with senior-level executives who are outside of their reporting structures.

• Asking successor candidates to step in and take over for other managers who, because of such factors as sick leave or reassignment to corporate projects, will be temporarily removed from their jobs.

All of these situations provide executives with opportunities to see successor candidates in action before critical job placement or promotional decisions need to be made, and to structure these learning situations in such a way as to provide one-on-one, in-depth coaching and guidance from more senior-level executives.

Finally, when you have the opportunity to identify long-term successor candidates for individual positions you are in a better position to compare your internal leadership capability against external talent. As an example, if you were able to take the time to line up two individuals whom you regard as being the strongest internal candidates to succeed your current corporate senior vice president of marketing, you could use this information to determine how these candidates would fare, given a hypothetical match-up against external candidates for the same job. In the television broadcast industry, this might mean conducting hypothetical comparisons of selected executive news directors or general managers against their well-known competitors in the industry. This type of targeted comparison isn't feasible when working with a large leadership talent pool.

Pitfalls Associated with the Stream Strategy

While the Stream Strategy offers the advantage of an intensive leadership development process, this process is also more rigid. By attempting to pre-identify successor candidates for individual leadership positions, you can end up forcing candidates into pre-slotted roles. The danger is that this slotting process can occur without considering whether successor candidates are willing to make the necessary trade-offs involved, such as moving into a position that is outside their skill sets, or relocating. At the same time, once certain leaders have been identified as appropriate successor candidates for certain positions, they may end up being pigeon-holed, and may fail to be considered for other, alternative development options.

A related problem is that the sheer effort required to conduct this identification process can result in the entire effort degenerating into a bureaucratic paper drill, with executives simply going through the motions of "completing the forms." If CTOs get overly ambitious, and attempt to force their organizations to record and track candidates for all leadership positions, little energy is left over to support meaningful development activities. Instead, the process ends with the filing of succession forms, and it quickly loses credibility with the management ranks.

Finally, if executives are allowed the leeway to select their own successors they will frequently focus on those direct reports who have been loyal supporters, and ignore (or be ignorant of) exceptional candidates who lie outside their work functions. In such a scenario, the use of the Stream Strategy will result in a limited review of sub-par successor candidates. To combat this problem, it is important to centralize the management of your successor process and involve both your CEO and other senior executives. Refer back to Figure 6-3 for assessment options that can prove useful in this assessment process.

The Pool Strategy

The talent pool concept is usually associated with a strategy of *continual recruitment*, in which exceptional managers are continually recruited without waiting for appropriate job positions to become available. Instead, such candidates are added to the general leadership talent pool and placed into temporary assignments until such time as appropriate positions become available.

When to Use the Pool Strategy

This strategy can be useful in the following situations:

• You work within a larger organization that has a broad base of talent from which to draw upon for promotional and successor candidates.

• Your leadership development efforts are largely geared to certain "keystone" positions. As an example, I know of a major office services company that focuses much of its high-potential activities on identifying managers for branch manager positions. By targeting this position, this company has generated exceptional talent pools for this designated area.

• Your company is in such a volatile business environment that it's difficult to predict your future organizational structure. In this scenario, designated succession planning may simply prove impractical, given that it will be difficult for you to predict career pathways for your managers.

Pay-Offs Associated with the Pool Strategy

The Pool Strategy supports the flexible deployment of leadership talent by insuring that there is a ready pipeline of pre-assessed candidates for a variety of leadership positions. Because executives can compare candidates on multiple performance criteria, they can run alternative scenarios regarding the comparative suitability of candidates for selected positions. This can help your organization respond much faster to changing conditions.

When leaders are identifying successors to key positions, this strategy also enables executives to look beyond their own limited pool of direct reports to evaluate the entire candidate pool, with the result that companies often fill positions with high-caliber candidates. At the same time, each pool participant is evaluated in terms of his or her potential for a variety of positions, resulting in more robust development planning.

Since larger organizations usually have access to a greater variety of developmental assignments and promotional opportunities, talent pools provide the additional advantage of allowing strong performers to be matched to a broad range of developmental assignments.

Another advantage is that when pool candidates are informed that they are being nominated for a high-potential pool, executives can engage them in honest discussions regarding any expectations their company might have regarding program participants. This might include the willingness to relocate, to adopt flexible career plans, or to display a strong interest in taking on broader promotional assignments. These discussions provide candidates with the option of self-selecting out of the pool, and help companies avoid wasting valuable time and resources on leaders who may not be a good fit to these types of programs.

A final consideration is that as a condition for entry into a talent pool, participants are usually formally reviewed, assessed, and evaluated, including an evaluation of their performance on short-term development assignments. This process introduces an element of safety in your succession and promotional decisions, by insuring that internal candidates are compared on a variety of performance factors before you make important judgment calls on them.

Pitfalls Associated with the Pool Strategy

The Pool Strategy comes with a big assumption, which is that pool participants share a common "fit" for the certain positions. This is likely to be the case for certain "keystone" positions that are critically important to your company and that require the same generic skill sets. Examples would include such positions as general manager, director of sales, and store branch manager. However, even these types of positions may hold subtle but important differences by location. Locations may differ by market size, by the size and complexity of the organizational structure, by the strength of competitors within those locations, by the presence of unique customer bases (such as the rapidly expanding Hispanic market), or by the strength of individual divisions or subsidiaries (strong growth, stable state, or turnaround situations). There may even be major differences in the personalities that make up the senior teams in different corporate divisions. (If you are identifying successors to fill positions within a very tough and competitive work environment, you may need to screen out those candidates would have difficulty surviving in a "shark tank.")

The key point here is that it is often difficult to design a uniform set of position requirements for your most important leadership jobs, given all of their myriad organizational manifestations. Accordingly, without some careful thought to this issue you could easily overestimate the degree to which pool participants can be interchanged across your organization.

A final thought is that the Pool Strategy provides greater "breadth" by sacrificing "depth." Participants in a talent pool often participate in a variety of developmental experiences, but these experiences seldom include intensive apprenticeships for targeted positions. With the Pool Strategy you may not have the luxury of implementing intensive development experiences that can allow successor candidates to be personally groomed for key positions by strong senior executives.

Working with Hybrid Models for HIPO Development

Some organizations have found it useful to combine the Stream and Pool strategies. In this approach, targeted successors are identified for positions above a certain organizational level, such as vice president– or director-level positions at the divisional level, and for all corporate officer positions. Positions that fall below these levels are filled through available talent pools. In fact, companies may find it useful to develop *multiple pools* for designated levels of development.

One of the largest office services in the United States uses this approach to develop one talent pool of high-potential, first-level managers as a pipeline for the branch managers in their stores. A second pool, comprised of selected branch managers, is then used to support the pipeline for higher-level executive positions.

When setting the development framework for HIPO pools, consider auditing your organization to identify the most important leadership development "jump points" that managers must bridge, in order to make a successful transition from one management level to another. Working in part from research originally conducted at GE, management consultants Ram Charan, Stephen Drotter, and James Noel, authors of *The Leadership Pipeline*, have constructed a leadership pipeline model that involves six key transition phases, or "passages," that managers must navigate along the leadership pipeline.[10]

These involve the passage from individual contributor to the levels of first-line manager, mid-manager (manager of managers), functional manager, business managers, group manager, and finally enterprise manager (president, COO, or CEO). For each transition point, the authors outline the associated leadership challenges that must be faced to make the jump to the next level. For example, during the fourth "passage"—from functional manager to business manager—leaders must learn to make the shift from the role of functional expert to taking a more strategic, longer-term perspective to the integration of multiple functions.[11]

One company that employs a variation of this model is Royal Philips Electronics, NV, which has identified three critical transition points for its HIPO leadership pool. These are the transition from being an individual contributor to becoming a leader of a high-performance team, the transition involved in learning to lead a business, and the transition involved in becoming a global leader of multiple businesses.[12] For each of these transition points, Philips has identified those factors that are most likely to lead to career stalls. For the executive who is attempting to make the transition into the role of being a global, multibusiness leader, such a career staller might be the lack of cross-geographical management experience.[13] The company's CTO and executive team work to provide their HIPO participants with targeted development support to successfully overcome these potential career stallers.

Collectively, this research points to a useful way of targeting the structure of high-potential pools so that participants are prepared to address their most important development challenges.

Notes

1. *Regarding the Full Potential of Rising Talent: Capturing Returns on the Identification of High Potential Employees,* Research Report (Washington, D.C.: Corporate Leadership Council, 2005).

2. Ibid, p. 29.

3. Ibid, pp. 32–33.

4. Ibid, pp. 36–38.

5. Ibid, pp. 30–31.

6. Helen Handfield-Jones, "How Executives Grow," *The McKinsey Quarterly,* June 15, 2000, pp. 116–123.

7. Ibid, p. 118.

8. *Unlocking the Full Value of Rising Talent,* pp. 93–95.

9. Ibid, pp. 88–89.

10. Ram Charan, Stephen Drotter, and James Noel, *The Leadership Pipeline: How to Build the Leadership Powered Company* (San Francisco, Calif.: Jossey-Bass, 2001).

11. Ibid, pp. 22–23.

12. *Unlocking the Full Value of Rising Talent;* Appendix, pp. 13–29.

13. Ibid.

CHAPTER 7

TALENT ACQUISITION DECISIONS

To seduce the enemy's soldiers from
allegiance and encourage them to surrender
is of special service, for an adversary is more
hurt by desertion than by slaughter.

—FLAVIUS VEGETIUS RENATUS
ROMAN WRITER AND MILITARY STRATEGIST

I believe that we've reached a point in talent management where most organizations understand the importance of investing in making effective executive recruiting and hiring decisions. That having been said, many companies still operate without a clearly thought-out talent acquisition strategy. Despite the huge impact that poor hiring decisions can have on organizational performance, quite typically senior executives and HR departments put very little thought into how they can best orchestrate their selection and interview process to raise their "hit rate" for leadership hires.

This problem reveals itself in a variety of ways. It's not unusual to walk into an organization and find that the company's leadership hiring process is poorly designed, with different departments and company divisions pursuing their own divergent, and some-

times contradictory, recruiting and hiring strategies. Executive recruiters may be hired and paid enormous sums without first being
required to pass through any sort of centralized quality review
process, or without being evaluated through even a cursory after-
action assessment to determine whether their recruiting efforts
have produced acceptable results.

In this scenario, executives have some vaguely defined concept
of what they require in the way of new leadership talent, but this
rough "gut feel" usually stops far short of accurate and detailed
talent forecasting. Recruiting efforts are initiated in a knee-jerk and
fragmented manner, and take form as individual, after-the-fact responses as leadership openings become known. In short, in this
type of hit-or-miss approach to talent acquisition, while the results
of some individual recruiting events may be exceptional, the collective, organization-wide impact of these efforts is frequently only
minimally effective.

The most important step that an organization can take to improve the overall effectiveness of its talent acquisition process is to
gain senior-level executive alignment on the goals of its recruiting
efforts. This chapter will show you how to use two talent acquisition decisions to gain that alignment.

The first decision requires you to decide whether your recruiting and hiring efforts are directed more towards improving the *size*
or the *quality* of your leadership bench. While you are likely to
argue that both objectives are equally important, I'd like to counter
by suggesting that most of us operate in such resource- and time-
limited work environments, that "doing both" just simply isn't an
option. Some organizations find it necessary to assume a Build-Out
Strategy, in order to quickly broaden their talent pipelines through
extensive broad-based, high-volume hiring efforts. Other organizations are more concerned with the very different objective of being
able to radically upgrade their bench. They attempt to do this
through the Trade-Up Strategy of replacing under-performing managers with significantly higher-caliber performers.

The second critical acquisition decision that you face involves determining talent sourcing, or how broadly across the marketplace you intend to scan for leadership talent. Some organizations believe that they are better off using the Best-in-Industry Strategy of seeking out the best performers from within their respective markets. Other companies cast a much broader net, and employ the World-Class Strategy to invest the additional time needed to import truly world-class leaders from across a variety of industries.

Considered together, these two talent acquisition decisions can guide you in determining the best way to focus your recruiting resources to meet the bench-building needs of your organization.

The Build-Out or Trade-Up Strategies

The Build-Out Strategy is quickly growing the leadership talent base by looking for ways to source, screen, and select a large group of managerial job candidates. By contrast, the Trade-Up Strategy is aimed at raising the overall performance bar for an organization's leadership bench, by "trading-out" bottom feeders (those managers who are performing at a marginal level) with top performers (see Figure 7-1). The strategy you select will significantly influence the resource investment needed to support your recruiting efforts, and the level of organizational change and disruption that will be incurred as a result of your hiring process. The decisions you make will set the stage for determining the degree to which your recruiting efforts will be measured in terms of operational efficiency, or the improved performance of your leadership bench.

The Build-Out Strategy

The Build-Out Strategy is intended for rapid growth, and is focused on hiring and on-boarding large volumes of leaders. The underlying assumption here is that your current leadership bench is quite strong and that you do can quite well by replicating the types of

Figure 7-1. The Trade-Up or Build-Out Decision.

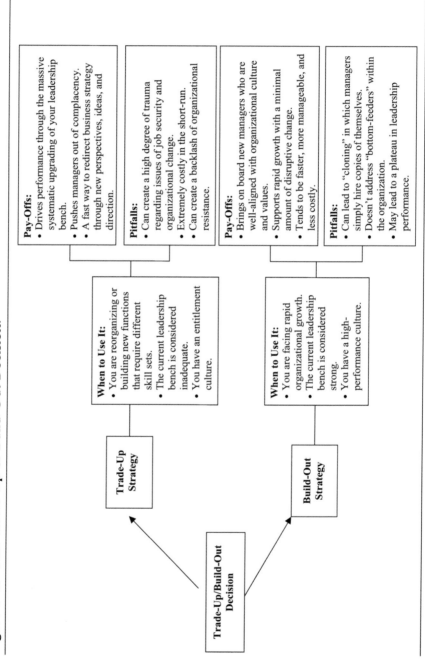

Trade-Up/Build-Out Decision

Trade-Up Strategy

When to Use It:
- You are reorganizing or building new functions that require different skill sets.
- The current leadership bench is considered inadequate.
- You have an entitlement culture.

Pay-Offs:
- Drives performance through the massive systematic upgrading of your leadership bench.
- Pushes managers out of complacency.
- A fast way to redirect business strategy through new perspectives, ideas, and direction.

Pitfalls:
- Can create a high degree of trauma regarding issues of job security and organizational change.
- Extremely costly in the short-run.
- Can create a backlash of organizational resistance.

Build-Out Strategy

When to Use It:
- You are facing rapid organizational growth.
- The current leadership bench is considered strong.
- You have a high-performance culture.

Pay-Offs:
- Brings on board new managers who are well-aligned with organizational culture and values.
- Supports rapid growth with a minimal amount of disruptive change.
- Tends to be faster, more manageable, and less costly.

Pitfalls:
- Can lead to "cloning" in which managers simply hire copies of themselves.
- Doesn't address "bottom-feeders" within the organization.
- May lead to a plateau in leadership performance.

leadership competencies, performance capabilities, and demographic composition that you currently have in place. A related assumption is that you already have in place a high-performance work culture, and that you are not attempting to undertake an organizational culture change that is so radical as to represent a difficult adaptation for most of your leaders.

When to Use the Build-Out Strategy

This strategy is more likely to be employed within one of two scenarios, the first being the enviable position of having to rapidly grow your leadership bench merely to keep up with exploding market demand for your services. As I write this, the big question in the investment community is whether the business start-up Google will quickly fall into this category.

In the second scenario, your organization faces the large-scale loss of part of your management team due to retirement or competitive poaching. There are many types of talent management challenges that this type of scenario can pose to an organization.

DEMOGRAPHIC CHANGES THAT CAN SPUR THE BUILD-OUT STRATEGY

Several years ago I was asked by a large federal agency to offer consulting advice regarding the changes that it could make to improve its succession planning process. I was brought into the agency by an HR colleague, an individual who had just completed a detailed demographic study of the top three levels of the agency's leadership team. The study showed that within ten years virtually 30 percent of this key leadership group would be eligible for retirement. A follow-up survey and interview process suggested that during the past several years many of these managers had weathered a series of stressful organizational changes, including staff reductions, which were now severely stretching their leadership capacity. Several interviewees admitted that they were rapidly reaching the point of burnout. As a result, a high percentage of these leaders indicated that they were more than ready to take advantage of the employee pensions that they had earned, and for which many of them would soon be eligible.

Another part of the study showed that due to the periodic expansions and contractions this agency had experienced in their staffing structure during the previous ten years (the agency seemed to grow or shrink with each new administration), the next two lower levels of leadership were filled by relatively inexperienced leaders. The bottom line was that my HR colleague and his agency's senior executives all concurred that they lacked the number of future senior leaders needed to fill the holes that would be left by the retiring managers. During this assessment and review process, the agency realized that it needed to go beyond its initial request for assistance on revamping its succession planning process, to engage the Build-Out Strategy. Given this conclusion the agency decided for the first time in its history, to develop an aggressive recruiting process designed to bring in large numbers of leaders from the outside.

Pay-Offs Associated with the Use of the Build-Out Strategy

There are several pay-offs associated with the use of this strategy. If you are confident in your assumption that you simply need to build out and replicate your existing management base, you'll be able to rely on a broad cross-section of your current management team to play a central role in helping you source, screen, select and on-board executive candidates. This scenario, of having established managers to help source, select, and on-board new talent, is more likely to yield a crop of new managers who are well aligned with your organization's culture and values.

In addition, since you are operating under the assumption that your recruiting strategy doesn't require you to identify, uproot, and replace a large group of poorly performing leaders, this scenario supports rapid bench-building with a minimal amount of disruptive change. The reason for this is that your managers are less likely to view incoming leaders a threat to their job security, or an implicit condemnation of their capability. After all, the Build-Out Strategy frequently takes place within an "expanding pie" scenario, in which you are struggling to keep up with your company's growth potential, meaning that there are more than enough new job opportunities for both experienced and incoming leaders.

In addition, since this scenario doesn't require you to raise the bar and search for job candidates that dramatically exceed the competencies and performance levels of your current leadership talent, it tends to be faster—and less costly *on a per-hire basis*—when compared to the Trade-Up Strategy.

Pitfalls Associated with the Use of the Build-Out Strategy

Recall that this strategy assumes that your organization can continue to strengthen your bench by simply replicating the quality of your current leadership team. In attempting to implement this strategy, most of the pitfalls that you face will occur when this assumption is faulty, that is, when your leadership team is either far weaker than you imagine, or comes up short with respect to being strong enough to help your organization tackle new and previously unanticipated business challenges. As mentioned in Chapter 6, this assumption is more likely to trip you up when you've been working within an insular organization that has managed to wall itself off from competitive review. An example would be a company that manages to carve out a market niche and to continue to grow for a long period of time, based primarily on the health of its internal talent pipeline.

Another drawback with this approach is that since managers tend to hire people like themselves, the Build-Out Strategy can produce a recruiting process that results in "selection cloning," in which managers simply hire copies of themselves. This can prove disastrous under several conditions. The first is when an organization realizes that during the next three to five years it will need to develop or acquire leaders who can work within a very different marketplace, using new technology, distribution channels, or product/service portfolios.

A current example concerns those traditional marketing functions that are attempting to bring on board the ability to use data mining to capture discrete customer segmentation. Such a pattern has been occurring over the past few years with large pharmaceutical manufacturers, as they attempt to arm their sales forces with information about the drug buying preferences of those hospitals, clinics, and private physicians that comprise their customer bases.

Selection cloning can also be a serious problem when an organization's customer base changes—by gender, age, or ethnicity—and when the organization lacks a leadership body that is representative of its changing customer base. A company that relies solely on its largely white, male executive team to attract, hire, and mentor women and minority leadership candidates is at a serious disadvantage to those competitors who make use of innovative and nontraditional recruiting sources.

Still another shortfall of this approach is that it doesn't address those "bottom-feeders" that tend to hide out in the nooks and crannies of the organizational structure. Bringing in good talent is fine, but keep in mind that when your recruiting actions simply add good players to weak players, over time your poorest performing leaders will continue to exert a strong drag on corporate performance. Moreover, if some of these poor performers will actually be managing the leaders that you are bringing in to your company, you set the stage for demoralizing and disengaging your new hires and for confusing them about the performance standards that you are attempting to put into place.

A final consideration involves the degree to which any organization can absorb rapid change. By its nature, the Build-Out Strategy calls for the large-scale importing of leaders from other companies and/or industries. Managing this influx of leaders requires careful thought as to what steps need to be taken to onboard them and help integrate them into your organization. The failure to do this can sometimes result in widespread resentment by the old guard, who may view the newly hired managers as representing a threat to their existing culture, status, and job security.

The Trade-Up Strategy

This strategy is typically employed within two very different talent management scenarios. The first scenario is when an organization is attempting to make a radical shift away from an entitlement culture, in which leaders have traditionally been rewarded for loyalty, seniority, and their ability to execute on clearly prescribed directions. Quite often, the change catalyst is a new CEO or president, who comes on board, raises the performance bar, and quickly determines that some of the current leaders are not strong enough to meet emerging business challenges. At this point, an aggressive external search, in the form of the Trade-Up Strategy, may be undertaken to find stronger replacements.

The Trade-Up Strategy is also employed when a senior executive team determines that while certain organizational leaders have the competencies and experience needed to manage the organization's *traditional* markets and products, they may not be fully equipped or prepared to lead that organization into a totally new business arena. In this situation, the Trade-Up Strategy is used not to search for stronger performers, but to search for leaders who can take the organization in an entirely new direction.

Pay-Offs Associated with the Use of the Trade-Up Strategy

The Trade-Up Strategy can drive improved performance through the systematic upgrading of your leadership bench. It involves importing exceptional leaders as replacements for mediocre managers.

The accompanying performance upgrade occurs not only because you've upgraded the quality of your leadership bench and have removed low performers who were creating a drag on performance, but because such actions usually serve as a wake-up call to those solid, but not stellar managers who have allowed themselves to become complacent. As they observe new leaders come in and quickly make headway on long-standing problems, long-standing managers become more willing to challenge the constraints and obstacles that (up until now) they've accepted as a natural part of the organizational landscape.

In addition, managers who are brought in through the Trade-Up Strategy often come in to the organization armed with a tough agenda for upgrading existing performance standards and metrics. By not only setting but also actively modeling such high standards, these new leaders force their teams to rethink what is achievable.

The trading-up of managers can also serve as a much needed source of adrenaline for those junior, high-performing managers who are anxious to work with, and learn from, exceptional senior leaders. In this way, the Trade-Up Strategy can serve as strong tool for supporting the retention of high-potential managers.

Pitfalls Associated with the Use of the Trade-Up Strategy

The Trade-Up Strategy is not without its drawbacks. For example, its use can create among incumbent managers a high degree of trauma related to concerns regarding job security and organizational change. If the new guard enters an organization in an arrogant and confrontational manner, it can create a backlash of organizational resistance, as more established managers find creative ways to block their initiatives.

This strategy can also prove to be very costly in the short run, both in the high compensation packages that will need to be paid to exceptional leaders, and in the severance packages that will be paid to displaced managers.

Another drawback with the use of this strategy is that it can pose a huge recruiting challenge for an organization. If a company is seeking to trade up to stronger performers because it has allowed its leadership bench to degrade over time, this fact will usually be obvious to the top players in the job market. The question, then, becomes how to "brand" a company as an attractive and challenging workplace, when the organization may not be respected within its industry as having a strong reputation for outstanding leadership talent. To counter this problem, CTOs are sometimes faced with making their offers more attractive to outside job candidates through large salary packages or inflated titles—a situation that can lead these candidates to hold inflated expectations regarding their possibilities for long-term compensation and career advancement.

Another issue involves carefully managing newly hired managers during their first few months on the job. In most cases, managers who are brought into an organization as part of a Trade-Up Strategy are tasked with being strong change agents for implementing tough performance standards, or with helping the organization reach out into new markets. The problem here is that these new standards or strategies may not be clearly communicated to the rest of the organization. Thus, the new managers can end up attempting to push change agendas without having the necessary organizational support and alignment. In some cases, employees may even lack a basic understanding regarding what constitutes the "new rules of the game." To address this problem, CTOs need to give sufficient thought as to how smooth the path for new managers by having senior executives explain to employees the business case for change, and the roles that new managers are expected to play in driving change.

How to Calibrate Your Leadership Bench Against External Performers

The type of talent management acquisition strategy that you select is based, in part, on how well you feel that your leadership team measures up to the broader pool of external job candidates. There is a danger here, in that quite often executives form assumptions about the comparative quality of their leadership teams without ever bothering to put these assumptions to the test. A common scenario is to assume that external candidates are far superior to your own internal talent pool and that you are engaging in a significant trade-up process, when you are in fact merely trading one set of reasonably good players for another. If you don't want to fall victim to this trap, and you'd like to obtain a more accurate comparison of how your talent stacks up against that your competition, consider taking the following steps:

1.   Shift from a "hire when needed" mode to the use of continuous hiring. Conducting frequent and detailed searches for exceptional leaders, even if you don't yet have open positions available, is one way to stay current on any changes, such as market contractions, that can significantly affect the quality of your external talent pipeline.

2.   Obtain third-party feedback. One great source for comparative purposes is your external customers. If a given department, such as sales, customer service, or distribution, represents a key contact point with your major customers, ask those customers how they feel that the quality of the services that you provide compare against those of your competitors. You might even consider going further and asking your customers to complete survey reports in which they compare your company's performance against your

competitors. You can use this information to determine not only how respective functions are faring in the playing field, but you can also draw from this data conclusions about the relative competence of your own managers.

Years ago when I was a partner in a management consulting firm, I would attend an annual supplier conference that was held by one of my corporate customers, a leader in the field of aerospace. After a nice pep talk and lunch, the head of the company's HR department would get down to business and discuss the comparative performance of our consulting companies. Each of us suppliers was given an envelope containing our own employee satisfaction scores, graphed against those of other companies who were identified only as companies "A," "B," or "C." I used this information not only to try to discover when and why we were trailing our competition, but as a comparative assessment process for evaluating the subcontractors that I employed on consulting projects with this company.

3. If you want to eliminate the "grass is greener" syndrome, try putting potential external job candidates to work. Give them a consulting project and see how they do. Don't limit this project to "conducting a study." Instead, put them to work helping you develop and actually carry out portions of an implementation plan for a key project—then see how well they co-manage the project with internal leaders. This approach can provide you with an incredibly rich array of data on the potential job candidate's technical ability and overall leadership and communication skills, as well as such factors as the candidate's ability to meet commitments, resolve difficult issues, and use influencing skills to enlist the support of your managers on key projects.

4. Look for examples of "best in class" work that might lead you to exceptional job candidates. As an OD practitioner, I'm continually reviewing professional journals and conferences in my field to see which OD professionals have received best practice awards, or who has authored articles on cutting-edge OD practices. This technique serves a dual purpose in that it can help you not only to identify potential job candidates, but to determine the degree to which your own managers are taking the lead in implementing industry best practices.

5. A related technique is to look for opportunities to see your internal managers in play against those of your competitors, through such avenues as trade shows.

6. If you are facing a situation in which you need to determine how the *overall* leadership team of one of your departments or functions compares to that of your competitors, consider staging a "fly-off" between your internal leaders and their external counterparts. This term comes from the airline industry, in which competitive suppliers are sometimes asked to put their respective new models through the same series of maneuvers in order to see which plane outperforms its counterparts. The following example illustrates how this kind of comparative review can be used to help you benchmark the performance of your leadership team.

Example: Using External Benchmarking to Assess Leadership Potential

A few years ago I provided talent management consultation to a privately held international logistics company. Three years prior to my involvement the company had launched its U.S. division, which included a sales function that was organized by five key geographical regions. Within each region, sales directors oversaw both new business development and large account management for a variety of corporate clients. The company's president—"Dave"—who had been brought on board two years before from another industry, strongly believed that the company's future growth was seriously limited by the organization's sales structure, and by a sales force that was woefully underpowered compared to those he had previously managed.

To complicate matters, while all of Dave's experience had been within U.S.-based companies, he was taking over the reigns of the company from "Tom," the former president who had been brought over from the United Kingdom. to direct the original U.S. launch. Once Dave had had been installed, the former president was retained in a senior executive position. Since Tom had been actively involved in many of the selection decisions for the company's sales force, it's easy to see why these two leaders didn't see eye-to-eye on many things.

Dave believed that some sales leaders tended to be good at "hunting" (aggressively capturing new accounts), while others were better at "farming" (maximizing account penetration on existing customers). Thus, in his view our company had ended up creating sales "sales mutants" who were only moderately capable of performing within both of these functions.

Based on these beliefs, Dave felt that many of his company's sales directors and leaders needed to be replaced by stronger external candidates. Tom, on the other hand, believed that we had in place the sales team we needed to succeed. After lengthy discussions with Dave, Tom, and the other members of the senior staff, I convinced Dave to hold off taking any drastic action until I had first the opportunity to evaluate our sales leadership bench. My goals were to develop a method that would enable us to identify our top-performing sales executives, while comparing the sales capability of our current sales team against external sales candidates.

Working with another consulting firm, we designed a three-phased sales assessment process. Over the course of the next three months we conducted over twenty in-depth interviews with senior-level sales executives and members of the senior team (including the president) to identify the competencies, experience, and knowledge required of the new sales directors. This data was then used to develop job interview questionnaires and a one-day sales assessment simulation. Over the next three months, all internal sales directors and external candidates (over seventy people, in all) participated in the sales assessment process, which evaluated their skills on such areas as the ability to develop a market strategy and to present a sales presentation to a mock customer team.

In addition, each internal and external candidate (incumbents were treated as job candidates and were required to formally apply for one of the new sales director positions) participated in a three-hour sales competency interview conducted by myself and (serving on a rotational basis) two senior vice presidents of sales. In setting up this process we set the guideline that no sales director could be interviewed by his or her own senior manager. As a final part of the assessment process, internal candidates were also compared on their revenue performance during the preceding twenty-four months.

All of this data was brought together for a one-day review that included Dave, Tom, myself, the rest of the senior team, and all five senior vice presidents of sales. At the end of that review, we had a much better idea of how the internal sales directors performed in relation to their external counterparts, and we were able to select top candidates for the new sales director positions. We ended up filling about 60 percent of the new sales positions from the incumbent sales force. The other 40 percent came from the external candidate pool. Many of the non-selected sales leaders were deemed more effective for assuming management positions in the newly created customer service function. Only a few internal candidates failed to make the grade to assume roles in either of these two new functions.

The assessment process seemed to have worked, for over the next twelve months the company recorded a huge improvement in its sales performance. An additional pay-off was that this process depoliticized the leadership selection and promotion process, by getting senior executives aligned on the key requirements for future sales leadership positions, by securing executive agreement regarding the relative importance of different sales director selection criteria, and by directly engaging a wide cross-section of the senior leaders in the assessment and selection process. Moreover, it provided us with a clear method for determining where our sales leaders stood in relation to their external counterparts. Finally, at the end of this process we were able to craft for each participant a detailed and highly relevant development plan, designed to help accelerate their transition into their new roles.

The Best-in-Industry and World-Class Strategies

The final set of acquisition decisions asks you to consider the most effective method for sourcing leadership candidates. The Best-in-Industry Strategy involves looking for the best performers from within your industry, while the World-Class Strategy involves investing the additional time and cost required to import world-class leaders from across a variety of industries (see Figure 7-2). The acquisition sourcing strategy you select has important implications for the structure and make-up of your leadership bench. It will also impact the types and levels of resources that you will need to employ in your recruiting efforts.

The Best-in-Industry Strategy

This strategy is based on the assumption that the pipeline for leadership talent in your industry is currently very strong, producing a large number of talented and qualified managers who are capable of helping your company meet anticipated business challenges.

When to Use the Best-in-Industry Strategy

This strategy is very attractive when industry-related experience is crucial to the success of your leaders, and when the lack of such

Figure 7-2. The World-Class or Best-in-Industry Decision.

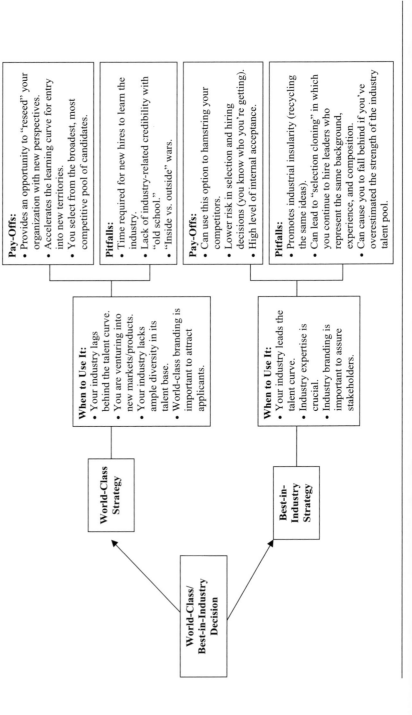

**World-Class/
Best-in-Industry
Decision**

**World-Class
Strategy**

When to Use It:
- Your industry lags behind the talent curve.
- You are venturing into new markets/products.
- Your industry lacks ample diversity in its talent base.
- World-class branding is important to attract applicants.

Pay-Offs:
- Provides an opportunity to "reseed" your organization with new perspectives.
- Accelerates the learning curve for entry into new territories.
- You select from the broadest, most competitive pool of candidates.

Pitfalls:
- Time required for new hires to learn the industry.
- Lack of industry-related credibility with "old school."
- "Inside vs. outside" wars.

**Best-in-
Industry
Strategy**

When to Use It:
- Your industry leads the talent curve.
- Industry expertise is crucial.
- Industry branding is important to assure stakeholders.

Pay-Offs:
- Can use this option to hamstring your competitors.
- Lower risk in selection and hiring decisions (you know who you're getting).
- High level of internal acceptance.

Pitfalls:
- Promotes industrial insularity (recycling the same ideas).
- Can lead to "selection cloning" in which you continue to hire leaders who represent the same background, experience, and composition.
- Can cause you to fall behind if you've overestimated the strength of the industry talent pool.

experience poses a severe disadvantage to new hires. An example would be a pharmaceutical manufacturer that is searching for outside candidates to fill leadership positions within its research and development department.

Pay-Offs Associated with the Best-in-Industry Strategy

• In many cases, this strategy can strengthen your own leadership bench while simultaneously hamstringing your competitors through the poaching of their best people. A related advantage is that such a move provides you with an insider track on competitors' moves. (Please note that I'm not suggesting asking newly hired executives to share information that would be considered to be proprietary to their former employers. At the same time, they may have insight into the overall direction and business priorities that have been set by those competitors—information that can help you anticipate and plan for competitors' moves.)

• This strategy can also be important for helping you develop "industry branding." For example, bringing on board executives who have "name presence" in your industry can be very important to such external stakeholders, as your customers and investors.

(Note: A hiring decision that illustrates these first two bullets occurred earlier this year when Ford Motor Company was able to woo away auto designer Freeman Thomas from DaimlerChrysler AG. While at DaimlerChrysler AG, Thomas had held the position of the director of the company's Pacifica Advanced Design Center. Many investors feel that Ford made this move because it recognized that innovative auto design is becoming a more important brand differentiator for car customers.[1] Of course it doesn't hurt that this defection may also pose design problems for one of their key competitors.)

• This strategy also lowers the risk for an initial hire, since it is usually easier to obtain a close-quarter view of industry superstars from others in your field in order to learn how those individuals performed in other companies.

• A related advantage is that leaders who are pulled from within your industry tend to have a faster learning curve, since they understand the business context for key decisions, the most significant competitors in your market (at least the traditional ones), and the dominant technologies.

• Industry superstars may also have established strong inroads with corporate clients in your field, a factor which can sometimes pay off in helping your organization expand its customer base.

• Finally, job candidates who are brought in through your industry tend to have a much higher level of acceptance and credibility from other managers in your organization, since they speak the same language and have proven their ability within a comparable field.

Pitfalls Associated with the Best-in-Industry Strategy

Earlier in this chapter I mentioned the problem of "selection cloning," in which executives tend to hire leaders who look, act, and think like themselves. As a general rule, selection cloning tends to pose a bigger danger for those companies that are attempting to follow a Best-in-Industry Strategy, as opposed to the World-Class Strategy, simply because the former strategy involves drawing job candidates from a more limited and homogenous talent pool. Thus, if the industry talent pool is not sufficiently diverse in terms of age, gender, or ethnicity, your company may have difficulty attracting and identifying a diverse pool of managerial job candidates.

The second way in which "selection cloning" takes form is that companies that draw job candidates almost exclusively from within their industries have greater difficulty bringing in leaders who can "think outside the industry mindset" and who can lead their organizations into totally new market areas. Some people credit the overwhelming success of the design and marketing of the iPod to the fact that Steve Jobs came from totally outside the music and entertainment industry. As a result, he didn't find himself bound by the dominant industry mindset that focused almost exclusively on creating barriers to the online dissemination of music, as opposed to looking for ways to mine online music distribution as a unique revenue stream. As a result, Apple—a computer company—has been able to take the lead in this new and exciting market.

Finally, the Best-in-Industry Strategy is effective only if you are correct in assuming that, when compared to other industries, your own industry has produced a strong leadership pool. By pursuing this strategy you are, in effect, placing a huge bet on the strength and robustness of your industry talent pool.

To be on the safe side, it is best to look outside your industry for independent sources that can help you objectively gauge the respective quality of the leaders in your industry. In my own case, I've moved into totally new industries several times in my career. Whenever I move into a new industry, one of the first actions that I take is to attempt to quickly determine the "floor and ceiling" for OD and HR talent within that industry. To do this, I typically use sources such as the Conference Board or the Corporate Leadership Council to determine how that industry fares in terms of the creation of leading-edge best practices. I've also formed contacts within some of the larger management consulting and executive recruiting firms who have been very helpful at helping me gauge the relative strength of OD and other leadership talent within my new field.

In your own case, you may have other sources that serve this function. The point is to look *outside* your industry to obtain a more objective assessment of the relative strength of the leadership talent that is being generated by your industry.

The World-Class Strategy

The World-Class Strategy is used when you attempt to seek executive job candidates from those organizations that have developed reputations as leaders in their respective fields, based on truly world-class standards. Accordingly, this strategy involves a very selective recruiting approach based on extremely rigid performance standards and selection criteria.

When to Use the World-Class Strategy

This acquisition strategy is likely to be used when you are attempting to fill a few key, high-level executive positions, and when industry knowledge is less important than having an exceptional track record as a business or organizational executive. It is an also an attractive strategy for those companies that are seeking to acquire staff for functional areas, such as human resources or IT, that tend to involve leadership and technical competencies that are easily transferable across industries.

This strategy may also be attractive for helping you address a broader range of leadership pipeline deficiencies, in situations in which you determine that your industry generally lags behind other industries in developing exceptional business leaders.

Finally, you may need to adopt the World-Class Strategy if your organization is venturing out into new territory, involving totally new markets or technology applications. In these cases, people within your industry simply may lack the necessary experience and creative mindset needed to help your organization set off in a new direction. Examples would include:

- A military subcontractor is taking its first steps into the commercial market.
- An energy company is attempting to shift from being only an energy producer to becoming both a producer, wholesaler, and energy trader.

- A "bricks and mortar" company is venturing out into Web-based marketing

- A procurement function is attempting to mutate from a traditional function of managing negotiations and quality control for company suppliers, to creating revenue-generating strategic alliances with other companies.

Pay-Offs Associated with the World-Class Strategy

The World-Class Strategy provides you with the many advantages that you would expect to obtain from a talent acquisition strategy that is based on extremely rigorous recruiting standards:

- This strategy helps you to identify leaders from across a variety of industries, who can provide your organization with new ideas and perspectives on products, markets, and technology applications. A related advantage is that the World-Class Strategy helps you dramatically shorten the learning curve for entry into new markets. An example would be a situation in which most of the players in your industry are currently constrained to the U.S. domestic market, and you hope to make your first move into the United Kingdom and central Europe. In this situation, it might prove more advantageous to bring on board leaders who have made their mark growing businesses in these markets, even if this move requires a trade-off in hiring people with less industry-related experience.

- The World-Class Strategy can be particularly helpful when the pipeline for leadership talent within particular functions is very sparse within your industry. If, for example, Web-based marketing is just beginning to take off in your industry, you may be better off searching for leadership talent within industries that have made significant in-roads in this area over the past few years. The same rationale applies when you are working within an industry that lacks ample gender, age, or ethnic diversity within its leadership base.

• If you are working in an industry that is not renowned for its leadership talent, adopting the World-Class Strategy may help you to bring on board the kinds of exceptional leaders who are needed to raise confidence in the investor community. At the same time, this move may also help you build the type of strong employment branding that is critical for attracting top-notch job applicants.

• By definition, the World-Class Strategy involves identifying leaders from the broadest, most competitive pool of external candidates that you can obtain. You then have the opportunity to load your candidate pool with the strongest leaders from within, and outside of, your industry. You can use your interview and selection process to compare the relative performance of these two different groups of candidates, and to uncover the different approaches that they might take toward solving your biggest business challenges.

THE WORLD-CLASS STRATEGY INTERNALLY FRAMED

An internal equivalent of the World-Class Strategy occurs when a global organization brings in someone from a totally different business unit or operation to head up an operation. A well-publicized example of this occurred early in 2005 when Sony Corporation took the unusual move to name Sir Howard Stringer, who formally ran Sony Corporation of America, as its chairman and chief executive officer. The move was unusual because Stringer is neither Japanese nor an engineer. He does, however, have a strong understanding of the entertainment business, which represents one of Sony's most profitable business operations. In commenting on this move, *New York Times* reporters Andrew Ross Sorkin and Saul Hansell said that Sir Howard "has tried to break through the bureaucratic logjams that have kept Sony—the company that invented the Walkman—

from competing effectively against Apple's iPod, the dominant digital music player."[2]

Pitfalls Associated with the World-Class Strategy

Being an incredibly selective and restrictive acquisition strategy carries with it a certain number of disadvantages:

• First, to attract world-class job candidates can be a very expensive proposition. If your industry is lagging behind others in the reputation of its leadership, you will have to work harder to build a strong case for attracting these exceptional candidates into your company. Often, that will mean offering bigger compensation packages and lofty management titles.

• A related problem is that although you are casting a bigger net for talent across industries, using this strategy could add months to the time required to screen and hire the right kind of talent. This will particularly be the case if you've been working exclusively with executive search firms that, while being experts on your industry, are relatively ignorant about how to focus their searches when extending themselves outside your industry.

• Given these first two issues, the World-Class Strategy is one that you may want to restrict to the identification of top-level leadership positions within your company.

• A big gamble here is the importance that you place on industry-related experience. Once again, you may find it helpful to make this judgment on a function-by-function basis, by looking for best-in-industry leaders to fill positions in core technical areas, such as operations or R&D, and casting a broader net for talent in more generic functions, such as marketing, IT, finance, and HR.

• Given their lack of industry-relevant experience, industry outsiders may not receive a positive reception from those leaders within your company who have grown up within your industry.

This problem will be exacerbated if you find that, in order to lure these world-class leaders to your company, you are forced to offer them much more attractive compensation packages and job titles than those provided to long-term employees. At some points in my career, I've encountered organizations in which this problem was so rampant as to lead to range-wars between the industry-insiders and their newly hired counterparts. If you think that you run the risk of incurring this scenario in your own company, give some careful thought to the steps you can take to minimize organizational "organ rejection" for newly-hired leaders. These steps might include the following actions:

- Creating a formal on-boarding program for managerial new hires to prepare them for your corporate culture
- Including a wider circle of influential managers in your selection interviewing process, to provide them with a sense of ownership in your hiring decisions
- Looking for job candidates who are able to build rapport, establish collaborative relationships with their peers, and build strong networks for influencing change
- Pairing newly hired managers with "old-timers," who can provide newcomers with advice and perspective on how to most effectively launch change initiatives

Additional ideas for helping leaders make transitions into your organization can be found in the two resources listed at the end of this chapter.[3,4]

Notes

1. Bill Koenig, "Ford hires former Chrysler designer," *Detroit Free Press*, May 2, 2005.
2. Andrew Ross Sorkin and Saul Hansell, "Shakeup at Sony puts Westerner in Leader's Role," *New York Times*, March 7, 2005.

3. Robert W. Barner, *Executive Resource Management: Building and Retaining an Exceptional Leadership Team* (Palo Alto, Calif.: Davies-Black, 2000).

4. Michael Watkins, *The First 90 Days: Critical Success Strategies for New Leaders at All Levels* (Boston: Harvard Business School Press, 2003).

CHAPTER 8

THE ART
OF DEPLOYMENT

Nothing is more difficult than the art of
maneuver. What is difficult about maneuver
is to make the devious route the most direct
and turn misfortune to advantage.

—SUN TZU, *THE ART OF WAR*

The best talent strategies are useless without solid execution. For
the talent strategist, execution takes the form of leadership deployment—the ability to leverage an organization's strongest leaders
against its biggest business challenges. Deployment is one of the
talent manager's most underutilized weapons. Many of us get so
caught up in analyzing the *front-end components* of talent management, such as leadership recruitment and assessment, that we fail
to stop and consider the critical role that's assumed by the *back-
end* component that involves the careful positioning of key leaders.
Furthermore, unlike such talent management functions as leadership development or executive assessment, managers seldom approach talent deployment as a carefully planned discipline.
Instead, many executives treat it as something that "just naturally
happens" through after-the-fact responses to changing events.

Why Deployment Is Important

However, as I'll discuss over the next few pages, there are several reasons why you should regard talent deployment as a critical lever for rapidly increasing organizational bench strength. The first of these is that *deployment releases the dynamic strength of your leadership team.* In making this statement I'm drawing an analogy from the game of chess, in which each piece is said to have both *latent* and *dynamic* strength. Latent strength refers to the optimal strength that a given piece can display on the board, while dynamic strength refers to the actual strength that the same piece has within a current board configuration. The point is that even the strongest chess piece, the queen, can have minimal dynamic strength if she is hemmed in by pawns. In the same way, an exceptional leader doesn't do you a lot of good if she is relegated to a low-value job in your organization, or is expected to learn and develop under the direction of a mediocre boss. I've seen numerous situations in which organizations have lost out on opportunities to improve their performance because they've allowed their star performers to languish in non-challenging roles that didn't make the best use of their talents.

In addition, *effective deployment provides immediate returns.* Unlike leadership development activities, in which there are frequently extensive time delays between implementation and the realization of pay-offs, deployment improves organizational performance almost immediately. The impact of a well-considered job redesign or a poor management placement decision reveals itself very quickly in terms of a shift in employee morale, retention, and organizational performance.

When effectively executed, *leadership deployment can yield synergistic gains.* That is, the promotion of a single, high-level executive into the right position can have a significant ripple effect on your organization by raising the performance capability of a function, while opening up additional opportunities to upgrade the caliber of leadership within several successive lower-level positions, through the judicious use of internal backfills.

Finally, and perhaps most importantly, *the inability to effectively deploy leaders can set severe limits on organizational growth.* An underpowered leader who is placed in a critical role can hamstring your operations, delay change initiatives, drive out star performers, and make bad hiring and promotion decisions that can fill your leadership ranks with mediocre talent. Left unchecked, allowing a weak leader to remain in a critical position can result in an incredible amount of damage in a relatively brief period of time.

The Seven Principles of Talent Deployment

I've intentionally avoided outlining detailed plans and prescriptions for talent deployment, since these will vary by circumstance. Instead, let me introduce you to seven management principles that have widespread applicability to a variety of leadership deployment situations:

1. Concentrate on the Critical Few
2. Determine Your Baseline
3. Employ Concurrent Design
4. Work Both Ends of the Spectrum
5. Make Your Timing Work for You
6. Be Sensitive to the Human Element
7. Adopt a Transition Plan

Principle #1: Concentrate on the Critical Few

You simply don't have the time and resources to ensure that all of your leaders are effectively placed across the board. Accordingly, give the lion's share of your attention to your most critical work functions. By the term "critical work functions" I mean those that

generate a high percentage of revenue, exert a high impact on overall costs, hold a central position in your organization's value
change, and are believed to play a key role in your company's future growth. If you manage a retail chain, these function may be
your marketing departments and those work groups that play a
role in managing and strengthening your supply chain. If you are
in a petrochemical company, these functions may involve those
petroleum engineers and geologists that direct your oil exploration
teams.

One word of caution here is that an organization's critical functions change over time. That is, you may be counting on new divisions or product lines to play a large role in your future success,
even though up to this point they've played only a minimal role in
helping your company grow revenue and market share. As a result,
don't rely solely on historical data to identify critical functions. Instead, engage your senior executive team in discussions on this
topic, with the goal of jointly identifying the 20 percent of your
organization structure that should receive the bulk of your talent
deployment efforts over the next three to five years.

Principle #2: Determine Your Baseline

Before you attempt to redesign part of your organization or move
your leaders around on the current chessboard, wouldn't it make
sense to first explore how effectively your leaders are currently
being deployed in your organization? This is a complicated question, but one that can be addressed by asking five other, more
targeted questions. Consider presenting these questions to other
members of your executive team, and using them as a catalyst for
gaining alignment on how best to deploy and engage your organizational talent:

- *Question 1: Are your best performers matched against your
most critical job categories?* Whereas work functions involve dis-

crete work groups that are directed against large blocks of work activities, *critical job categories* are those types of jobs that are central to the success of your key operations. If not properly filled, they can create huge problems for your company. For a pharmaceutical company, the most critical job categories may be the R&D directors and managers who are responsible for creating and testing new products. Typically, positions that reside within critical job categories tend to have a high market value, and the external candidate pools for them are very lean. Consequently, because it may be difficult to find qualified successors or replacements, when you start to suspect that job openings in these areas need to be filled, be certain to set aside more time than you typically would to conduct your search and recruiting efforts.

Taking this analysis a step further, consider that for any critical job category, such as a branch management position for a banking chain, leadership positions may vary in importance, depending upon the size and scope of their revenue or growth targets. To determine whether your best people are being properly deployed, ask the members of your executive team to take an important job category for your company, then rank the relative importance of all jobs within this category. As a second step, ask them to rank the performance of leaders who currently hold those positions. The results can be laid up on a two-by-two matrix to reveal areas in which leaders are being underutilized, as well as those areas in which underperformers have been ineffectively matched to critical job areas.

Figure 8-1 illustrates how this type of assessment might be applied to evaluating deployment patterns for a group of store managers for a hypothetical retail chain. The matrix shows how the store manager positions vary in importance, based on current average monthly revenue and the projected five-year market growth for customers in each location. In this example, we might begin to question whether our existing deployment process is very effective, given that we find only a moderate correlation between each store

Figure 8-1. Using a matrix to evaluate the effectiveness of leadership deployment patterns for store managers in a retail chain.

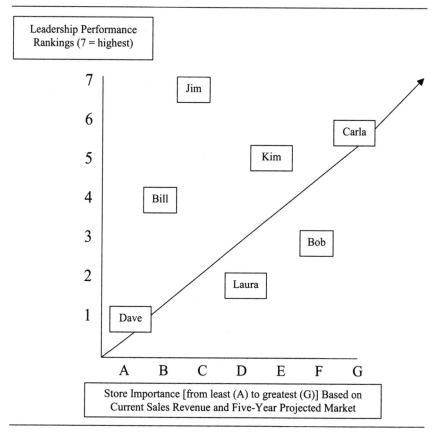

Leadership Performance
Rankings (7 = highest)

Store Importance [from least (A) to greatest (G)] Based on
Current Sales Revenue and Five-Year Projected Market

manager's competence and how they are being currently utilized. Obviously, additional questions would need to be asked, such as whether each manager has been in his position long enough to make an impact on factors such as employee churn, which can affect sales. However, once such factors are taken into consideration we should be able to draw important conclusions regarding the overall effectiveness of our deployment patterns.

• *Question 2: Do your best performers feel that they are being fully challenged on their jobs?* In other words, how are you doing on the retention of your best people? If you are not sure, do your homework and look at the percentage of leaders you've lost during the past twelve months who either (a) were rated as being exceptional performers on their last appraisals, or (b) had been identified as being high-potential managers. One caution here is to avoid relying rely too much on exit interview data, since departing managers tend to "say the right things" as they head out the door. Instead, use your informal networks to stay in touch with leaders who have recently left your company, then talk to them about their reasons for departing (off the record) after they have moved on to their new jobs.

• *Question 3: What effect has your current leadership deployment process had on your leadership pipeline?* Given that a good deployment process will be reflected in a strong leadership pipeline, take a look at such metrics (more on this in Chapter 10) as the time that's currently needed for your departments to fill open leadership positions, or the numbers of qualified candidates who are identified for open positions. A thin and emaciated leadership pipeline provides a strong clue that insufficient attention is being paid to deployment planning.

• *Question 4: How smoothly and seamlessly do deployment moves appear to be executed?* If people show up for new positions and have to wait a week to get hooked into your company's Intranet, or managers are given little advance warning to prepare for major leadership moves or transitions, then you can assume that your company leadership deployment is proceeding in a jerky fashion, with little or no advance planning or forethought. Keep in mind that an important part of deployment is "preparing the ground" for transplanting. Take a look at the process you have for culturally on-boarding new hires. Also determine whether you have an adequate process in place for helping newly-promoted managers clearly communicate changing performance expectations and changes in teams' charters and responsibilities.

• *Question 5: Has your company's leadership deployment process raised or lowered the overall quality of your leadership bench during the past twenty-four months?* There are two steps you can take to answer this question:

1. Track the performance of leaders on recent appraisals after they've been transferred or promoted. If many of your super-stars appear to "go nova" (e.g., encounter severe performance problems) soon after they've been repositioned, then you know that something is not working.

2. If you've taken the time to complete a leadership matrix, such as the one outlined in Figure 8-1, then you've already reached some conclusions regarding how well things are currently working. To make things more interesting, try rewinding the clock. Overlay the leadership matrix that you've prepared with a matrix showing the leaders who held each of these positions two years ago. Now compare the two lists. Has the overall caliber of your talent base improved during this time? Are your leaders better positioned (the strongest leaders being placed against the most important positions) than they were two years ago?

If you can't answer "yes" to both of these questions then you need to take a serious look at your leadership deployment process.

Principle #3: Employ Concurrent Design

Managers have traditionally tackled talent deployment as a series of disjointed decisions that are made on an after-the-fact basis, as positions become open. This same patchwork approach treats organizational design decisions as entirely separate from decisions regarding talent deployment. That is, whenever a new business initiative is proposed or plans are underway for making extensive changes to business processes or functions, executives are usually well into their design decisions before they bother to ask, "Who do we have on board who can run these operations?"

In contrast, the concept of concurrent design means simultaneously evaluating both the organizational design options at your disposal, and the actions you have available for strengthening leadership capacity. This approach allows you to look ahead and determine the talent you need to have on board in order to build, acquire, or restructure organizational units to meet projected goals.

You can easy see that engaging in this type of approach can help you spot critical leadership shortfalls. However, concurrent design yields additional advantages that extend well beyond this obvious feature. For example, this approach can also be used to help you evaluate the alternative tradeoffs of various bench-building options, including the respective constraints, risks, costs, and speed of implementation that are associated with each of these options. It also allows you to fully exploit unforeseen opportunities.

EXPLOITING UNFORESEEN OPPORTUNITIES FOR LEVERAGING TALENT

A few years ago I was attempting to help a company beef up its sales and marketing function. At one point, we uncovered an executive candidate for a national sales director position who also happened to have had prior experience in a business start-up in Mexico. The candidate's international background afforded us a unique opportunity to help accelerate a pilot launch in that country. As a result, we negotiated an employment agreement in which this executive agreed to spend approximately 25 percent of her time over the first six months on site in Mexico to coach and advise our pilot group, while spending the bulk of her time building the national sales network. As an additional pay-off, a year later when it came time to scan the organization for leaders who could assist with a similar launch for another country, this sales director proved invaluable in providing us with feedback on the leadership capabilities of each of the leaders in the Mexico launch.

As illustrated in Figure 8-2, the starting point for making use of concurrent design is to establish forums that encourage your senior executives to engage in the simultaneous discussion of strategic initiatives, organizational design, and leadership capacity.

One area in which this type of integrative review is increasingly seen is in the changing nature of the annual leadership talent review (LTR). LTRs have typically been limited to discussions about the relative strengths and weaknesses of key organizational leaders, as viewed within the current business context. In contrast, these leadership management events become true tools for talent strategy development when they expand to include discussions about the organization's *future* talent capacity. In this approach, HR leaders and senior executives discuss organizational leaders through the lens of hypothetical "what-if" scenarios, to consider how those leaders are likely to perform against future constraints and opportunities. (Additional information on this subject is provided in Chapter 9.) Thus, the question talent strategists ask is not, "How do we evaluate this leader's potential to meet existing job challenges?" but rather "How would we evaluate this leader's potential to succeed three to five years down the road, given the radically transformed business landscape that we envision?"

While LTRs provide the most obvious opportunity for concurrent design discussions, these types of discussions can be initiated whenever you find yourself facing important decisions regarding your organizational structure or leadership bench. All that is needed is your willingness to stop and consider how each decision point you face may raise secondary opportunities for improving organizational performance. Figure 8-3 provides several examples of the types of cross-fertilization that can be generated between the components of organizational structure and leadership talent.

Figure 8-2. Using concurrent design to leverage leadership deployment.

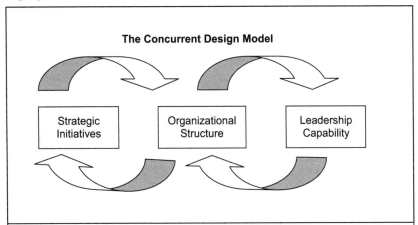

Concurrent design allows us to explore the broadest range of options for fulfilling strategic initiatives:

- What's the optimal organizational design for supporting this key initiative?

- In evaluating our leadership bench, to what degree do we think we have in place the talent we need to meet this business challenge?

- How can this business initiative provide unique development opportunities for our top performers?

- Is there some way to modify our initial organizational design to take advantage of the unique experience and competencies that our leaders bring to the table?

- What are the most significant leadership shortfalls that we face? Left unaddressed, how might these issues affect our likelihood of success on this new initiative?

- What is the optimal timing for implementing changes to organizational structure and talent deployment?

Figure 8-3. The synergies created by linking organizational design and talent management activities.

Organizational Design Options	Actions for Strengthening Leadership
• "Our Financial Planning and Financial Analysis functions would perform more effectively if they were brought together under a single manager."	• "That could serve as a great opportunity for Carlos. He's ready to take on broader responsibilities."
• "You're right. The question that I have is whether we even need the senior director position. What if we used this opportunity to eliminate all three position and focus more accountability at the Director level?"	• "David will be retiring next year. Rather than simply replacing him, why don't we rethink what this means to our sales operations?"
• "That's why I've been considering whether we should place Sarbanes-Oxley compliance under her as well. Her background is stronger than the manager we currently have on board."	• "We think that Kim is going to be a great addition to our team. Apart from her great background in accounting and finance, she also has prior experience in a corporate audit function."
• "We can get greater operating efficiencies if we can centralize our IT functions and work to a common platform."	• "That makes sense, but we need to think about who could step up to that position. We need someone who is strategic, and who has experience in systems integration."
• "What if we assigned her to Bob? She could learn a lot by working with him, and the product development experience that she brings with her would help him greatly on that new customer segmentation project."	• "Galena isn't going to learn a great deal under Karen. If we don't want to lose Galena we might want to think about moving her under a much stronger manager."

Before we move on I need to present two caveats. First, it may be that, within your company, decisions regarding organizational change and those regarding leadership talent are guided by two different HR functions. If this is the case, you'll need to work as a broker to bring the leaders of these two functions together for discussions on this topic. One way to do this is to give each of these individuals a copy of this book and ask them to be prepared to discuss with you the ideas presented in this chapter, with particular attention to the concept of concurrent design. Getting their initial assumptions and biases on the table can be the first step to a fruitful discussion on this topic.

Second, while concurrent design can afford the savvy talent strategist with a variety of advantages, if this concept is misused, it can backfire with disastrous results. One type of misuse is when executives attempt to force-fit talent decisions to quickly secure changes to organizational structures. Consider the case of an engineering executive who was brought in to head up a mechanical engineering function. During the course of the job interview the hiring manager discovered that this engineering leader had significant experience in Six Sigma quality improvement. Soon after this individual was hired, the head of the engineering department decided that this executive represented a great opportunity to launch the company's first Six Sigma function (a move that had been under review by the company for the past several years). The newly hired executive was adamant that he didn't want to take on this role, but in the eyes of the executive team this opportunity was too good to pass up. Unfortunately, the executive quickly became frustrated with this new arrangement and opted to leave the company, resulting in the needless loss of a great talent.

The opposite situation can also occur, when organizational design considerations are compromised to accommodate the personal needs of certain managers. A few years ago I encountered a situation in which a customer service director—"Jim"—was nominated by his executive manager to participate in an exclusive company-wide development program for high-potential leaders. I challenged this decision, based on the fact that the manager's performance in his function had been less than exemplary. The senior executive's response was, "Well, that was Jim's current job, but that situation is changing. We've decided to split his function in half to make it more manageable for him. Another manager will now be handling all of the call center functions. Given this new development, we feel comfortable listing Jim as being a high-potential leader since that we think that he'll have the potential needed to succeed in his new role."

The moral of these two stories is to avoid force-fitting linkages between organizational structure and leadership talent. The rule here is, "If it doesn't fit, don't force it."

A special application of concurrent design involves working to ensure that your talent infrastructure components, such as performance appraisal and executive compensation, are well aligned with your talent goals. Figure 8-4 provides a template that can be used to systematically review this question, while Figure 8-5 provides an illustration of how the model could be applied to an organization that is attempting to strengthen its leadership bench within its business development function.

Principle #4: Work Both Ends of the Spectrum

When it comes to leadership deployment, executives typically focus their attention on the top end of the spectrum; that is, determining where they can place their best managers to obtain the best performance from them. However, a sometimes overlooked aspect of deployment is in developing plans for dealing with an organization's poorest performers. When these "bottom-feeders" hold critical management positions they can do a great amount of damage to an organization, not just through their own poor performance, but through their poor talent decisions. The simple fact is that a mediocre manager can't be counted upon to be able to identify top

Figure 8-4. A template for aligning talent goals with talent infrastructure.

Talent Infrastructure Assessment Chart

Talent Goal	HR Talent Infrastructure Components						
	Performance Management Process	Executive Compensation	Strategy Communication	Executive Recruiting	Executive Assessment	Executive Development	Organizational Design
Impact: Positive, Negative, Neutral, or Unknown							

Figure 8-5. Aligning talent goals to talent infrastructure for business development teams.

Talent Infrastructure Assessment Chart

Talent Goal	HR Talent Infrastructure Components						
	Performance Management Process	Executive Compensation	Strategy Communication	Executive Recruiting	Executive Assessment	Executive Development	Organizational Design
To significantly upgrade the leadership talent in our business development teams	*Neutral*	*Negative*	*Positive*	*Negative*	*Unknown*	*Positive*	*Unknown*
Impact: Positive, Negative, Neutral, or Unknown	Current PA process appears to be fully adaptable to this need.	Best-in-class companies appear to allocate more money to incentive bonuses here. We are currently well under market.	Focus group feedback indicates that all management groups understand the importance of this activity to our goals for market growth.	Our current recruiting team has little experience in this area.	We need to benchmark our generic assessment process to evaluate its applicability; what will our "hit rate" be, using our current approach?	We appear to out front in our industry in this area.	Consider funding a recruitment research group to benchmark possible organizational designs, staffing patterns, and reporting structures.

talent, to create tough performance expectations that encourage talent growth, or to help junior-level managers to develop over time. In addition, consider the adverse effects that poor performers can have on employee morale.

Still another factor is that your poorest performers are typically your most change-resistant leaders. The reason for this is that individuals who tend to squat in the center of their comfort zones and resist change find it difficult to adopt best practices, to stay on top of changing business conditions, or to keep current on key technical skills. Finally, keep in mind that, whether you like it or not, many junior-level managers may inadvertently begin to model the performance of your worst leaders, under the mistaken idea that if their bosses hold positions of influence in your company they must be doing something right.

Here are a few suggestions for managing the deployment of your worst performers:

• Before taking any action, make certain that you have all your facts straight. If you have serious doubts regarding the performance of some of your managers, consider supplementing all available performance appraisal reviews with additional data sources. Included here would be 360° data, interviews with internal or external customers, available outcome metrics (such as revenue figures for a sales manager), and conducting discussions with second-level managers to see how they view the performance of those leaders who have been identified as being "poor performers." Give special attention to input from your divisional and corporate HR teams, who probably have additional background information that they can bring to the table, and who can provide needed guidance in making "coach or cut" decisions on these performers.

• Ask yourself whether you have the data needed to distinguish between four types of managers:

1. Those who simply don't put in required effort and need to be terminated.

2. Those who are obviously mismatched to their jobs, but who may be able to provide value if they are matched more appropriately to other jobs in your organization.

3. Those who have targeted skill deficiencies and good self-insight into their own performance deficiencies, and who could benefit from coaching, training, and management support.

4. Those who exhibit strong patterns of "derailment" behaviors, such as borderline ethical behavior, arrogance, insensitivity to others, resistance to change, or the failure to adapt to new conditions and expectations. These individuals represent borderline situations, where tough decisions must be made regarding the leader's amenability to coaching. (Note: For additional information on career derailers, check out the online list of publications available through the Center for Creative Leadership [www.ccl.org].)

• Give special attention to identifying areas in which entire work groups may be improperly deployed. Quite often this occurs when, as a result of shifting business needs, a work function is asked to step up to a very different set of work responsibilities, to master a completely different set of technical skills, and to be held to more demanding performance standards. In this case you may find that the people who work within a function just can't take you to where you need to go. Here are some examples:

• Recall the example of the procurement function introduced in Chapter 3. In that situation, many people in the procurement department simply couldn't make the jump to master the responsibilities required to direct a strategic alliances function.

• I know of an entire corporate marketing function that was replaced because it had, for years, limited its expertise to such areas as managing trade exhibits, staging customer events, and generating promotional collateral. When a new

CEO came on board and realized that the marketing function lacked the skills needed to provide targeted data on the changing preferences of the company's customer base, he was forced to gut most of the team and start over.

- It's quite common for service departments—such as finance, IT, and HR—to go through this type of soul-searching when they attempt to make the transition from transactional service organizations to becoming strategic business partners. A by-product of such transitions is usually an attempt to automate or outsource the more routine work functions.

Principle # 5: Make Your Timing Work for You

In talent deployment, timing is a critical factor. Over the past few years I've witnessed several powerful examples of how important it is for leaders to understand the sensitivity of timing in executing leadership talent moves:

- I know of one company that had developed an excellent recruiting and development program for newly hired external managers. Unfortunately, it took the company three years to develop a comparable program for its internal high-potential talent. In the interim period, the incumbent managers resented the recognition that was given to these "outsiders," and the company lost an opportunity to send clear signals about the value it placed on its internal leadership.

- One of my colleagues in another company shared with me a story regarding a well-loved executive who was simply unable to help his department adapt to new business conditions. As a result the manager, who was close to retirement, was "eased out" and a younger, more aggressive replacement was brought in from the outside to replace him. Unfortunately, the timing of these moves was rather slipshod, and the new manager was brought in without taking the proper steps to recognize and acknowledge the efforts of the exiting manager, who was even forced to come in on a Saturday to clean out his desk. These actions created a huge wave of employee resistance to the incoming manager, who didn't discover these series of events until after she had joined the company.

• I know of one company that invested heavily in a formal, university-sponsored executive development program that was custom-designed for its branch managers. The problem was that the company lacked solid coordination between its talent management function (which developed the program) and its organizational development and HR functions. As a result, the design of the executive development program didn't take into consideration the dramatic way in which the branch manager's role would change following a major reorganization. A few months into the program delivery it was scrapped, resulting in needless cost to the company and the loss of credibility for the talent management function.

In considering the timing of your own deployment moves, try to identify any organizational changes that could affect the success of your deployment actions:

• Do you really want to be launching a formal leadership development program during an organizational reduction-in-force?

• Does it make sense to schedule the head of a work function for a four-week, offsite advanced management program when her second-in-command is due to be out during that period for extended medical leave?

• If, as a work-related development action, you want to transfer a junior-level manager into your corporate finance department for three months, wouldn't it make better sense to wait until the new CFO has been hired and is sufficiently grounded to ensure that the manager gets a good mentoring experience?

When planning leadership deployment actions, these are the types of questions that you should ask yourself. When engaging in this thought-exercise you might also find it useful to ask for advice from your CTO, the head of your HR department, or other executives who have a clear view into the timing of major organizational events.

Principle #6: Be Sensitive to the Human Element

In making deployment decisions, one of the great dangers that CTOs face is to ignore the human element. The leadership talent decisions we make have subtle repercussions that extend beyond the balance sheet, to include how individuals interpret these actions in terms of power, prestige, and the expression of key organizational values. This means that before we engage in a serious deployment action, be it transplanting a work function from one facility site to another, or extending a development opportunity to a junior-level manager, it is important to think through the alternative ways in which those actions are likely to be interpreted by others in our organizations. Once again, while I don't have a step-by-step plan in my pocket, I can offer up for review the following general guidelines:

• Always assume that at least 20 percent of the message that you are trying to communicate will be lost or distorted as it is repackaged and communicated at each successive lower level in your organization. So, if you are trying to explain your rationale for launching a new leadership development initiative, or for reorganizing a part of your company, there is a good chance that four levels below you, the underlying messages that you are trying to drive home about your leadership standards, corporate values, and your future expectations of leaders aren't getting through. The only way that you can combat this problem is to over-communicate. Use a variety of formats to send your messages, including e-mail, memos, and face-to-face meetings.

• As a general rule of thumb, the more emotionally sensitive the message, the more you will need to rely on a communication mode that is personable, informal, and which encourages two-way discussion. When communicating important messages pertaining to talent management, never lead with a memo or e-mail. Once in circulation, these vehicles tend to have lives of their own. As a result, you'll end up spending most of your time attempting to follow-up on communication breakdowns or rumors, as the communications are passed along from one manager to the next. Instead, lead with a series of cascading face-to-face discussions, starting with your more senior executives and working down each successive level.

• As another rule of thumb, the more emotion that is baked into a talent deployment decision, the more you need to *slow down in your communications* and take time to listen to people and allow them to vent. Over the years I've witnessed many managers who have been labeled as cold and uncaring because in their haste to resolve emotional issues—such as severing a long-time, well-loved employee—they didn't make the effort to spend a few extra minutes to express at least a minimal amount of caring and empathy.

• Never assume that the good intentions behind your deployment decisions will be automatically understood by others. Instead, build an informal check-and-balance into your own decision-making process. Look around your organization and identify those two or three managers who appear to have the ability to maintain balanced judgment in emotional settings, and who have also built a strong base of influence and support in your organization. Use these mavens to help you identify points of resistance for potential leadership changes. For example, before you consider reaching down into your organization to quickly promote that newly hired junior-level manager into a much higher management position, ask your mavens, "How is this change likely to land in our organization?"

• Be honest. Never mislead. The ultimate fulcrum for organizational change is trust. If you have a large amount of trust in your emotional bank account, when it comes time to make a difficult change you will find that others in your organization will assume that you are not operating from a personal agenda, but rather have their best interests at heart.

• Sometimes we make the mistake of feeling that when communicating tough decisions, its best to "get to the bottom line." Let me propose an alternative view. When attempting to implement a difficult deployment change, don't just describe *what* will change. Go further to *explain why* your company is doing this, the *long-term impact* that the change will have on your organization's long-term performance, and *the thought process that went into this decision.* This provides organizational members with a solid way of framing and interpreting your actions, and will give them a greater appreciation for the effort you put into the decision process.

Principle #7: Adopt a Transition Plan

Deployment isn't a simple on-off switch; that is, you don't make a decision and proceed immediately from one organizational state to another. Whether you are talking about replacing an executive, upgrading a function, or streamlining a department, the talent deployment actions that you set into play take time. The bigger the change to structure or staffing, the longer the delay that's involved. It is during this transition period that things can get a little crazy. While you are waiting to finalize a small reduction-in-force, morale can sink. The aftermath can be that good people become overly anxious regarding their own job security, and jump ship before you have the opportunity to put in place adequate retention actions. In the same way, between the time that you've terminated a poorly performing executive and are conducting a search for a replacement, you could experience serious erosion in the affected function's overall performance.

To avoid these types of organizational distress, once you've made a decision to make a significant change to your structure or leadership staffing, you should immediately set out to create a detailed transition plan. Such a plan can help you anticipate some of the potential pitfalls that can emerge during organizational transitions. In addition, by asking other executives and HR leaders for their feedback and suggestions, your plan can also serve as common roadmap for gaining team alignment on how you can most effectively proceed through these changes.

CREATING A TRANSITION PLAN TO SAFEGUARD THE MANAGEMENT OF CUSTOMER ACCOUNTS

Earlier, in Chapter 3, I shared an example involving the reorganization of a logistic service company's sales department. In that situation, directors who had managed both customer service and sales activities for corporate accounts were reorganized into two different departments, one being sales and the other being customer service. This move required changes to reporting structures and bonus incentive plans, and the relocation of several directors to new locations. Moreover, it also meant that in many cases directors had to turn their sales and customer service accounts over to other directors.

To safeguard the process of transitioning customer accounts, our department created a detailed "transition template" that our directors could use to create their own customized transition plans. The template asked them to describe the steps that they and their counterparts would be taking over the next sixty days to facilitate the transfer of accounts to other managers, the role that each incumbent manager and new manager would play in managing communications with customers during the transition phase period, the time-frame for the shifting of accountabilities, and how the incoming and outgoing directors would manage communications involving the purpose, timing and steps of the transition process.

When developing your own organizational transition plan follow these six steps:

1. Estimate the likely time period between the start of the change and its completion. For example, consider the situation in which you've decided to replace a mediocre performer with a stronger external candidate. How long will it take you to find a suitable replacement, negotiate an offer letter, and bring this person on board? When generating these types of time estimates, be conservative; most people err in giving overly-optimistic estimates regarding the time that they will need for hiring or transitioning managers.

2. Now overlay your projected time-line over your corporate calendar and ask the question, "What *else* will be going on in our organization and industry during this time that could dramatically impact the success of this project?" As an example, you may be planning to reorganize your sales function, only to find that during the same time your company will be coming up for renewal for several contracts with corporate customers. As another example, you may find that your plan for rapidly growing one of your departments happens to coincide with the time that all of your HR recruiters will be sucked up into a major corporate HR project.

3. Other useful questions to ask are: "What other business initiatives that have strong stakeholder support will be underway during this time period? Which of these initiatives could provide needed 'air cover' for our talent initiatives?"

As an example, assume that you have the goal of launching your company's first enterprise-wide 360° leadership assessment.

At the same time, you may know that your senior executives have strongly advocated having your HR department undertake a company-wide employee retention and satisfaction survey. In this situation, you might time the launch of the 360° assessment to immediately follow the release of the retention survey. In this way, you could sell the 360° assessment, in part, on the grounds that the feedback that you'll receive from your 360° reviews can help you determine whether certain low-retention work functions also have leaders who exhibit certain types of dysfunctional, non-supportive behavior.

4. For each step, consider what could go wrong, including peripheral fallout in the form of lower employee morale, retention risks, the unanticipated loss of resources, or resistance to certain aspects of your planned changes from other work groups or departments.

5. Consider actions you could take to manage potentially disruptive factors, such as:

- Find ways to shorten transition time. In the case of our executive replacement, this might involve interviewing executive search firms, establishing your search criteria, and having the firm that you select provide you with an initial review of candidates during the last sixty days that your incumbent manager is employed with your company.

- Identify back-up actions that you could take to avoid painting yourself into a corner. In my own case, before launching a new management development program, I always attempt to have other employees and outside consultants trained to backfill for me in order to provide greater flexibility in program delivery.

- Ask several senior managers to "smooth the path" for you by stepping out ahead of certain critical steps to communicate their support of the project and help you address potential points of resistance.

6. Look for ways to "prepare the ground" for leadership moves. If you are planning to hire a new manager, hold detailed, candid conversations with your executive recruiter and job candidates regarding the unique characteristics of your organizational culture. Share with them examples of leaders who have performed well in your company and those who, although technically proficient, may have bombed out because they failed to adapt their leadership style to the prevailing culture. Also, take the time to explain to incoming managers the symbolic value that small leadership actions may have in your organization. Here are a few examples:

- In some companies, talking on a cell phone or playing with your Blackberry during staff meetings is viewed as being arrogant or insensitive. In other companies, it is viewed as a natural part of doing business.

- Some organizations thrive on e-mail. In other organizations, although e-mail is commonly used, when managers need to give critical feedback or push back on issues they are expected to pick up the phone and work it out directly. Sending e-mail "flames," or needlessly escalating issues by sending copies of hostile e-mails to one's boss, are considered to be unnecessarily confrontational.

- In some organizations, it is considered extremely important to join in on after-hour social events or to inquiry about an individual's family, while in other companies leaders erect very high firewalls between their work and their personal lives.

- In some organizations, leaders who are viewed as strong, independent, and assertive are expected to come into staff meetings prepared to defend their plans from harsh criticism. Leaders who wilt in these types of discussions are dismissed as being ineffective wimps. In other organizations, attacking others' ideas in staff meetings is considered a sign of poor teamwork, and the managers who display this kind of behavior are viewed as hostile and overly aggressive.

My point is that every company is different, and organizational participants are quick to form assumptions about newcomers based on these types of behaviors. Accordingly, take the time to sit down with new managers during their first few days on their new jobs and engage in detailed on-boarding discussions, in which you lay out the informal norms and expectations that define "good leadership" for your organization. The same goes for those managers who are promoted or transferred from one organizational unit to the next, since every operating company and department tends to have its own distinct work culture.

A second step you can take to prepare the ground for managers who are coming into an organizational setting is to provide them with the background and context needed to understand the work team's history. It might be helpful for a manager to know that the members of a work group are beginning to feel burned out as the result of an extremely heavy work load, before bringing the group together to give them a lecture about the need to work harder and hit higher performance goals.

An executive who is coming into a work team from the outside might find it useful to know that she was selected over two members of the current work team, who are now feeling very demoralized, and who have been talking openly about leaving the company.

Before the newly installed leader engages in a head-butting conflict with one of her reports, she may find it useful to know that this report has been a long-term friend of the executive vice president who heads up their business unit.

The point is that woven throughout every organizational unit are a variety of invisible threads and trip-wires. Take the time to keep newly installed managers alerted to these contextual issues. Also, help them locate, within their teams, leaders who will be willing to pull them aside occasionally and serve as a sounding board for discussing these types of issues.

CHAPTER 9

CONDUCTING WAR-GAME SCENARIOS

If I appear prepared, it is because before
entering an undertaking, I have meditated
long and have foreseen what might occur. It
is not genus which reveals to me suddenly
and secretly what I should do in
circumstances unexpected by others, it is
thought and preparation.

—NAPOLEON BONAPARTE

After reading Chapter 8, you may have come away with the mistaken idea that once formed, the execution of a talent strategy always proceeds along a fixed and predictable path. This traditional view of strategic planning calls to mind the image of some sage general who, looking down from a clear vantage point high above the battlefield, is able to easily predict how his troops, weapons, and resources can be best deployed. However, if you stop to think about it, this war metaphor doesn't quite work. Actually, the most effective generals in history, such as Napoleon, were those who were able to seize the moment and quickly take advantage of shifting circumstances. When we envision the future, not as a straight and invariable path, but as a series of probabilities and potentialities, we become much more alert to hidden threats and opportunities that could impact our planning process.

The Importance of Staying Flexible

This premise holds equally true for the talent strategist. Should the right opportunity present itself, you have to be willing to adopt your initial talent management plans to changing conditions. Here are a few examples:

• *Creative Poaching.* A few years ago I worked as a talent management consultant to a large aerospace company. This client was smart enough to see a competitor's downsizing activity as an incredible opportunity for importing exceptional talent. As a result, even though such a recruiting action hadn't been built into our original game plan, we adapted that game plan to take advantage of a unique situation. The competitor's HR leader and I worked together to go after some of the company's recently terminated executives. We then used these executives to capture additional leaders from this competitor who, prior to this point, were not actively "in play." The success of this project was due to this company's ability to aggressively seize a talent management opportunity when it came their way.

• *Recalibrating Talent.* A senior-level sales executive, who was challenged by his manager to come up with a plan to make substantial improvements to top-line revenue, used this initiative to shift his company to a more consultative sales approach. Based on this approach the executive mapped out a very different sales competency model. He then used this model as the criterion for reevaluating all company sales directors and managers, getting rid of a lot of dead wood in the process.

• *Preventing Recruiting Problems.* A commercial shipping company had set the goal of rapidly expanding into the Caribbean market. In reviewing this plan, the company's head of HR and the CEO were very concerned that this plan could be potentially derailed by the lack of strong, talented leaders within its field offices. An underlying problem was that the company lacked a seasoned recruiting director who could help them strengthen their leadership bench. Upon realizing that it might take several months to land the right director, the head of HR contracted with a local, recently retired HR executive to initiate their recruiting process, and help them develop a more detailed and comprehensive view of their field strength. At the same time, they hired an executive search firm to initiate the search for a permanent recruiting director. Six months later, the company still had not found the right player through their external search efforts. The good news was that, during this time, their contract recruiter had performed so well that the company brought the contractor on board to lead their recruiting efforts. This contingency plan provided them with a way to jump-start their recruiting efforts while engaging in a low-risk assessment of a potential job candidate.

• *Fully Leveraging Top Players.* A division president needed to reorganize her company to prepare it for its first expansion outside of the United States. Rather than simply develop a plan to reshuffle existing players into the new structure, the president used this opportunity to consider how to make more effective use of her top VPs. The resulting restructuring eliminated several assistant vice president positions, and saved the company quite a bit of money. More importantly, however, the new structure eliminated levels of needless bureaucracy, while streamlining decision making and making full use of the capabilities of her top players.

Why War-Game Scenarios?

To test their military readiness, generals make use of war games or simulations, while chess masters spend many hours planning out potential responses to potential moves by their opponents. In the same way, effective talent strategists know the importance of conducting simulated "war games" that test the adaptability and resilience of their talent strategies against certain change scenarios. Thus, scenarios can be used to prepare for the types of talent challenges that could occur following a reorganization, or entry into a major market. War-game scenarios can be used to prepare for positive scenarios, such as the possibility of bringing on board a world-class leader, or potential negative scenarios, such as the potential acceleration of voluntary terminations immediately following a company-wide reduction-in-force (RIF).

It is important to understand that there is a significant difference between engaging in scenario building and creating a corporate vision. When organizations strive to create a compelling vision of the future they are attempting to put together a clear, coherent picture of how they want their company to perform in the future. Scenario building doesn't deal with *a desired future*; it offers up *several alternative futures* in the form of detailed stories or scenarios.

To better understand this concept, consider the following analogy: A mechanical engineer might be asked to employ the concept of robust engineering to design an all-terrain vehicle that is capable of performing in a variety of environmental conditions. In a similar fashion, a talent strategist might use data on a company's emerging business conditions to help construct future scenarios that test the robustness of targeted talent management strategies. To do this the talent strategist asks the question, "Is the approach that we've identified to build our bench strength sufficiently adaptable to a variety of potential future conditions?" The answers to this question are then used to refine and strengthen the organization's leadership talent strategy.

Advantages of Scenario Planning

There are several advantages to engaging in this type of scenario development:

• *You are better able to anticipate problems or opportunities that might otherwise remain overlooked.* If you are considering potential candidates to replace a leader who may be leaving your company in a few months, scenario planning encourages you to broaden your scope of inquiry and identify candidates from across your company who might not otherwise be considered. Even better, you may view this leader's departure as an opportunity for completely rethinking how his operation is currently organized, and for considering organizational redesign changes that could improve the effectiveness of this function.

• *Scenario planning helps you to manage complexity.* In scenario planning, you don't simply consider how one potential change event could affect an organization. Instead, you evaluate the consequences of the interactions of multiple factors. Rather than view the future in terms of discrete data bits, scenario planning asks us to tell rich, detailed stories about the future that would be hard to assimilate with traditional, linear planning.

• *Scenario development enables you to respond much faster to disruptive changes.* Many large-scale talent management actions require not only a huge commitment in resources, but also concurrent changes to company policies, incentive compensation plans, and the creation of continuity plans for keeping work efforts high during transition periods. All of these things take time. By using scenario development to plan ahead, you can smooth the path for these changes and substantially shorten their time for execution.

As an example, if you think that there is even a small chance that you will need to mobilize for a new market launch in six months, wouldn't it be prudent to set aside contingency funds for hiring and relocation costs now, while you are in the middle of your annual budget planning process? Going further, wouldn't it make sense to get the selection of an executive recruiting firm out of the way now, so that if you do decide to launch, you've helped these recruiters to plan ahead by arming them with detailed position descriptions and criteria for candidate selection?

• *Scenario planning lowers the risk level for decision making.* You can also use this technique to explore the likely outcome of events. In addition, occasionally this technique can provide you with a low-risk method of testing tentative decisions before you are fully committed to them. A classic example involves developing an exclusive partnership with a university or outside vendor to create management training for your leaders.

Scenario planning might lead you to consider how you could go about creating a "taste-test" of a proposed program before committing to a pilot, and to consider which company locations would yield the most useful information from these pilots. In addition, such actions also provide you with opportunities to "test-drive" relationships with external suppliers, to determine the degree to which they're able to meet commitments and deliver quality service, *before* you are forced to commit major funds to an extended program.

• *Scenario development allows you to make more carefully considered decisions.* Without the use of preemptive planning, when a major change occurs executives may feel pressured to make expedient decisions that don't serve the long-term interests of your organization. Through scenario planning, you can carefully weigh alternative talent management options and gain executive alignment on key decisions, before you find yourself caught up in the middle of an emotional, stressful change.

• *Scenarios can help you gain alignment on future actions and clarify points of resistance.* In going through the process of detailing their scenarios, executives are able to focus more clearly on the many business and leadership assumptions on which their visions of the future are based. By making these scenarios clear and explicit, people find that they are more readily examined and put to the test, and discarded if they are subsequently proven to be invalid.

• *Scenario planning makes you more sensitive to emerging trends.* The act of constructing scenarios forces you to identify those trend lines and trigger events that signal the emergence of a given scenario. As a result, leaders who engage in scenario planning are more likely to note and accurately interpret the full significance of those lead indicators that signal the onset of an important change, much like the way a stock analyst might note the full meaning of a sudden shift in a stock's performance indicators.

• *Finally, engaging in war-game scenarios develops your ability to think strategically.* In most fields of competitive play—whether we are talking about a military campaign, football game, or chess game—there is a danger in restricting our attention to a single area of the playing field. Good players attempt to keep the entire field in view. In much the same way, when we participate in scenario development we are more likely to consider the broader ripple effects generated by a single leadership deployment action.

For example, when we need to fill an opening we are more likely to think about other leadership openings that will eventually need to be filled and ask ourselves whether it makes more sense to conduct these moves in tandem. We are also more likely to consider talent deployment actions from the simultaneous perspective of how those actions translate into short-term gains to organizational effectiveness, and long-term gains to the development of certain leaders.

Scenario planning can take a variety of forms. In the remainder of this chapter, we will deal with deal with two different applications to talent management. The first of these, *the "what-if" talent scenario*, helps you to think through the potential business impact of changes to your leadership bench. In contrast, you can use *business scenarios* to determine how adaptable your current talent strategy is to broader business or organizational changes. Figure 9-1 illustrates the differences between these two scenario applications.

Figure 9-1. Differentiating between two types of change scenarios.

What-If Talent Scenarios ask: "To what degree could the following changes to our leadership bench affect the performance of our organization?

Key Change Events that Alter Bench Strength	→	Resulting Changes in Organizational Operations	→	Resulting Changes to Organizational Performance

Business Change Scenarios ask: "To what degree are our talent management strategies adaptable to potential environmental and business changes?"

Changes in Environmental Conditions or Business Factors	→	Resulting Changes in Organizational Operations	→	Test the Resiliency of Our Talent Management Strategies

Application #1: Using "What-If" Scenarios to Evaluate the Business Impact of Changes to Your Leadership Bench

This "what-if" scenario approach asks you to consider the broader impact of a single, short-term change event on your organization. "What-if" scenarios have been used to explore both positive change events and negative change events:

Positive events might include such questions as:

• "What would happen if we were able to successfully recruit this particularly candidate, who is trilingual and has extensive international experience, into our executive rotation program? This represents a unique set of skills—how would we make the best use of this opportunity?"

• "Could we use this planned reorganization to rethink the current management structure of our customer fulfillment center? What types of leadership skills would be needed to support the new, proposed organizational structure? How might this new structure generate new leadership development opportunities?"

Negative events could include such questions as:

• "What would happen if Jennie is lured away next year by that competitor who keeps coming after her? How would this impact her work team? Might anyone on her team follow her to her new job? What actions could we take to prepare for this?"

• "What happens if we seriously underestimate the numbers of managers who take us up on the early retirement offer that we are going to be initiating next month? Hypothetically, what would the loss of an additional 20 percent of all eligible managers mean to our leadership team?"

You can easily see that with a few minutes of thought you could generate for review an unmanageable number of scenarios. Therefore, the challenge you face becomes determining how to pare this number down to the three or four events that merit your attention. One useful technique involves going back to the process that was introduced in Chapter 8 for identifying critical work functions and positions. For each of these critical functions and positions, you can then attempt to generate a list of potential changes to your leadership talent base.

A final step involves generating a list of preemptive and supportive actions. *Preemptive actions* are actions you can take *in advance* of the change event that serve to better prepare you to deal with it. *Supportive actions* are those change management actions you can plan to take *during* the course of the event, should it actually occur. Figure 9-2 shows the "what-if" analysis that might be constructed for a potential retention issue having to do with the loss of a key team member. Note that under the "potential impact" column we've included both potential negative ($-$) and positive ($+$) outcomes that could proceed from the event.

Application #2: Using Business Scenarios to Test Talent Readiness

This use of scenario building involves working with other executives to identify those critical business and industry changes that could significantly affect your organization's overall performance, then working backwards to assess your talent readiness for meeting these changes. In this way, the scenario process helps you to test the resilience of your talent strategy. Another way of expressing this is that business scenarios help you to determine the probability that your current talent strategy will enable you to meet your long-terms goals, regardless of the different ways in which business conditions could unfold in the future. This form of business scenario development consists of the following five steps:

Figure 9-2. Creating a "What-If" talent scenario chart to address the potential loss of a company director.

The "What-If" Talent Scenario Chart

Talent Change Event	Potential Impact	Preemptive Actions	Supportive Actions
Loss of Jennie Star, our director of New Business Development, to a competitor over the next twelve months.	− Potential six-month delay in our acquisition review of Delta Corp. − Potential loss of S. Smith and D. Gupta, Jennie's NBD Managers. − S. Smith would need to step in as interim manager, preventing her planned promotion to our DIS division. + Might be an appropriate time to consider merging our New Business Development and Business Analysis Departments.	• Recommend that D. Gupta co-manage with Jennie the next phase of our acquisition review of Delta Corp. • Use informal networks to determine competitor's growth requirements in NBD (how many people will be coming on board?) • Implement a retention bonus for Jennie. • Ask the EVP, Finance to conduct a career development meeting with her. • Conduct "check-in" discussions with Smith and Gupta. • Craft a contingency plan for accelerating the departmental reorganization (who would be essential to the post-organized department?).	• Have SVP, Strategy, and Financial Analysis directly manage Smith and Gupta. • Request that Thompson delay his retirement for a few months, to support Smith's delayed promotion to the DIS division.

1. *Select a business or industry change for review.* If you attempt to explore all potential change scenarios, you'll soon find yourself overwhelmed by change. The key to narrowing down your field of review is to first consider which two or three business drivers have the greatest volatility, and are most likely to impact the performance of your company over the next three to five years.

2. *Identify potential future outcomes.* Starting with one of these business drivers, attempt to determine the most optimistic and pessimistic future outcomes for this factor. Next, describe what a "mid-range" outcome (one that resided half way between the two extremes) would look like. Now complete this process for a second business factor. Finally, since scenario building is all about looking at the interactivity between factors, construct a Scenario Matrix, such as the one shown in Figure 9-3, for capturing this information.

If other organizational leaders will be providing input into your scenario, I recommend that a week prior to meeting together you give each of them six blank note cards. On three of the note cards, ask them to describe how they would view the most optimistic, pessimistic, and mid-range outcomes, should one of these factors occur. Then ask them to use the remaining three cards for describing their anticipated outcomes for the second factor. Before you meet again, draw Figure 9-3 on a flipchart. Then during your meeting, ask them to determine where, within the nine cells of the chart, they would like to place each card. As a team, review the

Figure 9-3. Scenario matrix for two interacting events.

Scenario Matrix		Three Alternatives Futures for Event 1		
		Situation 1	**Situation 2**	**Situation 3**
Three Alternative Futures for Event 2	**Situation 1**	Scenario I	Scenario II	Scenario III
	Situation 2	Scenario IV	Scenario V	Scenario VI
	Situation 3	Scenario VII	Scenario VIII	Scenario IX

placement of the cards to determine where participants agree on future outcomes, and where they hold different views of the future. This simple exercise provides a means for participants to obtain a detailed, shared view of possible futures, and how they view the connection between large-scale changes and organizational impact.

Figure 9-4 shows a completed matrix for "Alpha-Gamma," a hypothetical clothing boutique that specializes in high-end leisure apparel for young women in the 18-to-34 age group. Since Alpha-Gamma is attempting to market through its stores and, concurrently, its newly established online website, its executive team has selected for review two factors that they believe will strongly influence the success of the company's online business. The first factor (represented by the three columns) is the expansion of online sales as a percentage of all sales revenue, or how fast online sales are expected to grow relative to overall sales.

In addition, realizing that they are a young company that hasn't yet built a powerful clothing brand, Alpha-Gamma has decided to accelerate its sales by forming unique partnerships with other online stores, to support the cross-promotion of products and to drive additional customers into their Web portal. Accordingly, the second, related factor that the executive team has chosen for study (shown in the three rows) is the percentage of online sales revenue over the next three years that may be derived from partnership agreements with other online sales companies.

The interactions of these two variables produce nine scenarios. To provide ready reference to these alternative futures, each has been given a name, which is shown in the cells in Figure 9-4. What the team would also generate would be a one-page briefing sheet describing the characteristics that would most likely be associated with each scenario.

3   *Determine the relative importance of each scenario.* To help focus your attention, you can then create a second matrix (shown in Figure 9-5) that allows you to sort the nine scenarios by proba-

Figure 9.4. Completed scenario matrix.

Scenario Matrix: Three-Year Time Horizon 2007–2010	Three Alternative Futures for Event 1: Expansion of Online Sales as a Percentage of All Sales Revenue		
Alternative Market Scenarios for "Alpha-Gamma" Clothing Boutique	**Situation 1** Pessimistic: Online sales expand to no more than 10% of all sales revenue within three years.	**Situation 2** Mid-range: Online sales expand from 15% to 25% of all sales revenue within three years.	**Situation 3** Optimistic: Online sales grow from 5% of total sales to 35% of total sales.
Three Alternative Futures for Event 2 Percentage of online sales revenue derived from partnership agreements with other online sales companies			
Situation 1 Pessimistic: We fail to obtain a partnership agreement, and 100% of sales are internally generated.	Scenario I *Minimal Entry Scenario*	Scenario II *Home-Grown Scenario*	Scenario III *Busting Loose Scenario*
Situation 2 Mid-Range: 50% of sales come from partnership agreements with other companies.	Scenario IV *Leaning Out Scenario*	Scenario V *Steady State Scenario*	Scenario VI *Solid Growth Scenario*
Situation 3 Optimistic: 80% of sales come from partnership agreements with other companies.	Scenario VII *Outsource Scenario*	Scenario VIII *Big Brother Scenario*	Scenario IX *Double-Win Scenario*

Figure 9-5. Mapping the importance of potential organizational scenarios.

Impact of Scenario	High	C	B	A
	Medium	C	B	B
	Low	D	C	C
		Low	Medium	High

Probability of Occurrence for Scenario

A = Critical Events that Merit Immediate Attention
B = Events that Merit Careful Consideration and Continuous Monitoring
C = Events that Merit Periodic Review
D = Events You Can Ignore

bility and impact. Based on these two factors, the resulting nine-squared matrix can be broken down into four levels in terms of relative importance, with these levels ranging from critical events ("A") to events you can ignore ("D"). According to the level of interest, each scenario merits a different degree of time and attention.

4. *Perform a talent readiness assessment.* Starting with the "A" scenarios, ask yourself how, if a given scenario came to pass, it would affect your future needs for leadership talent. In other words, what would be the size and composition of the leadership team that you'd have to have in place in order to meet each of these potential work challenges? What unique competency and experience profiles would be expected of your leaders? A related approach involves asking whether, given your current bench strength

and the talent strategy that you currently have in place, you feel that you are ready to meet the future business challenges represented by each scenario.

   5. *Identify plans for addressing critical scenarios.* This might involve adapting your current talent strategy to these future conditions, or adopting different talent management actions within your current strategy. For example, to prepare our "Busting Loose" scenario we may find that, as shown in Figure 9-6, we have to convert from a "Make" to a "Buy" talent strategy. This will enable us to broaden our search for talent by beginning to look outside of our business unit and across our entire enterprise for potential candidates.

Additional Suggestions for Managing Talent During Conditions of Uncertainty

In closing this chapter, let me share with you six guiding principles that may prove helpful when you are attempting to build your talent bench under conditions of uncertainty:

   1. *Think small and modular.* An oil tanker is certainly the most economical way to transport oil, but let's face it—it's a little difficult to turn around at sea. In the same way, when you are operating under conditions of uncertainty, you don't want to lock yourself into massive five-year talent development programs. The trade-off here is that you may have to be willing to give up some of the efficiencies of scale that you'd normally expect to accompany an organizational commitment to a large-scale training or consulting contract. Instead, be willing to pay a little more for programs that can be quickly supplemented or transformed to meet new business conditions.

   2. *Keep your resources fluid.* In the same way, during unstable conditions it makes more sense to meet growing demands for tal-

Figure 9-6. Determining the talent impact of critical business scenarios.

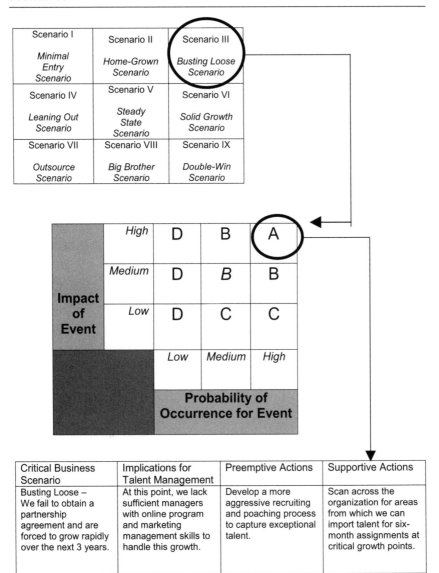

Critical Business Scenario	Implications for Talent Management	Preemptive Actions	Supportive Actions
Busting Loose – We fail to obtain a partnership agreement and are forced to grow rapidly over the next 3 years.	At this point, we lack sufficient managers with online program and marketing management skills to handle this growth.	Develop a more aggressive recruiting and poaching process to capture exceptional talent.	Scan across the organization for areas from which we can import talent for six-month assignments at critical growth points.

ent management services through the use of contract support than by adding on additional staff. Contract arrangements allow you to trade off or replace contractors to meet sudden changes in service requirements.

3. *Learn to implement faster.* I came into one company a few years ago that was attempting to stage a financial turnaround. During the first months on board, the new CEO and EVP of HR fired the existing CTO. One of the reasons given was that this leader simply couldn't move fast enough, as shown by the nine months of effort that he had invested in developing the company's leadership competency model. A high-change scenario is not the time to get stuck in analysis paralysis. Instead, work with your executive team to make certain that you know what their expectations are regarding speed of execution. In addition, look for ways to conduct "fast prototyping," or the use of quickly formulated models and pilots to accelerate program execution. If, for example, you are attempting to launch a new leadership development program and are exploring multiple content formats, what's wrong with staging simultaneous pilots and follow-up evaluation studies to move faster to implementation?

4. *Build in check-in points with your stakeholders.* When launching a detailed talent management project, red circle those points on your Gantt Chart where you expect to encounter the greatest areas of uncertainty and risk. Build into these points brief check-in calls with your senior stakeholder group, so that you can keep them alerted to time-periods in which you may have to make quick adjustments to your plans. Explore those options ahead of time and get approval, in advance, for any contingency plans that may have to be executed to secure your talent management goals. Examples would include the extended use of external resources, or the shifting of project responsibilities from corporate to divisional HR sites.

5. *Hire learning agile people.* If you are operating in a highly unstable environment, the last thing that you need to contend with

is a CTO, or someone in a talent management support role, who requires a high degree of structure and guidance. Give special consideration to bringing onto your team individuals who are able to adapt quickly to fast-changing business conditions. During your job interviews, ask candidates to provide you with examples of situations in which they tried to implement talent management plans and found themselves faced with drastic changes mandated by their senior management, or encountered several changes to their organization's business outlook. Try to determine how well these job candidates were able to bounce back when they encountered setbacks and unforeseen difficulties.

6. *Learn from others' mistakes.* One of the best ways to plan for uncertainties that could derail your bench-building initiatives is for you to conduct "post-mortem reviews" with organizations that have already gone through the change events that you are about to encounter. These events might involve such things as implementing an enterprise-wide talent management software system, designing your company's first succession planning, high-potential, or mentoring program, or determining the guidelines and practices that you would need to put into place to get the most out of a 360° multi-rater feedback system. The point is not only to uncover best practices, but also to ask three questions that can help you capture the "lessons learned" distilled from the other organizations' experiences:

1. "What took you by surprise?"
2. "Looking back, if you were about to undertake this project again, what would you do differently?"
3. "At what point in this project did you encounter the greatest wave of organizational resistance?"

I find that this approach has saved me from a lot needless pain, by helping me think through key issues before they are encountered. Using this approach also encourages me to make more realistic plans for resources and time commitments to projects. In addition, if you can create opportunities for the leaders of other organizations to share their learning experiences on talent management projects with other managers in your company, you can use these events to queue up discussions on the relative effectiveness of alternative approaches to talent management initiatives.

CHAPTER 10

KEEPING SCORE

However beautiful the strategy, you should
occasionally look at the results.

—SIR WINSTON CHURCHILL

One of the most common reasons that talent management strategies fail is that CTOs and their executive teams fail to periodically evaluate the effectiveness of these strategies. Even in cases in which such tracking is attempted, CTOs and executives don't always employ metrics and measures that are clearly defined and well-aligned with their organizations' overall talent management objectives.

Performance Metrics: Your Organizational Compass

There are several reasons that the construction of effective metrics is essential for the success of any talent management process. First, a solid evaluation process serves as a conceptual compass for focusing organizational attention. You can't, for example, determine whether you are improving in the performance area of "retaining top performers" unless you are able to clearly define leaders who meet the criterion for being "top performers" (your

203

metric), and how you evaluate leaders in terms of this dimension (your measure). In addition, a common set of clearly defined metrics helps to keep the disparate efforts of different organizational members, operating companies, and departments focused on a few critical measurement factors. In the same way, having a common set of metrics allows you to compare the progress being made on bench-building efforts across different organizational units.

Finally, keep in mind that the evaluation measures you select send strong signals to your organization about how you define the "success" of bench-building programs. For example, you could define success in terms of "pipeline yield metrics," such as the percentage of internal leadership positions that are filled internally rather than through external hires. The use of such a measure will direct your talent management efforts along a very different pathway from such alternative measurement approaches as evaluating the quality of leadership placements (e.g., "the percentage of external or internal job candidates who are performing in top appraisal categories twelve months after hire, or after promotion into new positions").

If performance metrics are important, the question then becomes how to make them work for you. I recommend that you concentrate on five talent management actions. As illustrated in Figure 10-1, these actions relate to five hurdles that you need to jump in order to design and implement effective leadership talent metrics:

Step 1: Ensure That Metrics Are Relevant and Valid

The metrics that you select should be very relevant to your talent requirements. At first this might seem so self-evident as to seem unworthy of discussion. After all, what executive would bother with a performance metric that didn't meet this criterion? However, it's important to realize that whether they intend to or not,

Figure 10-1. Jumping the five hurdles that accompany the creation of talent metrics.

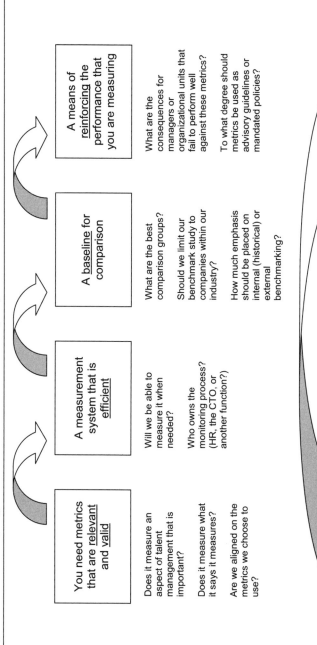

You need metrics that are relevant and valid

Does it measure an aspect of talent management that is important?

Does it measure what it says it measures?

Are we aligned on the metrics we choose to use?

A measurement system that is efficient

Will we be able to measure it when needed?

Who owns the monitoring process? (HR, the CTO, or another function?)

A baseline for comparison

What are the best comparison groups?

Should we limit our benchmark study to companies within our industry?

How much emphasis should be placed on internal (historical) or external benchmarking?

A means of reinforcing the performance that you are measuring

What are the consequences for managers or organizational units that fail to perform well against these metrics?

To what degree should metrics be used as advisory guidelines or mandated policies?

Organizational stakeholders must be aligned on how metrics and measures will be employed.

Do we agree on the approach that we intend to employ to measure and evaluate the effectiveness of our talent management efforts? Do we agree on who will collect this data and how it will be used?

organizations sometimes invest a great deal of time measuring talent management activities that are only marginally related to their long-term, bench-building goals.

To better understand this, assume that you are working in a highly competitive industry in which there is such a demand for leadership talent in some areas that leadership retention has become a big issue. You plan to address this by having your managers complete an annual organizational employee satisfaction and retention survey, and then use these scores as a bellwether to help you target those work functions or departments that may be the most vulnerable to retention risks. As a secondary metric, you've decided to track the percentage of voluntary terminations that occur for all managers and executives within each work unit.

These metrics sound good but are they really relevant? Do you really care about the retention of *all* of your leaders—even the poorest performers in your organization? A more telling metric would involve identifying, as separate leadership subgroups, your solid performers (those who continually meet or exceed performance expectations), and the partially overlapping group comprised of those managers who have been identified as being high potential leaders. You could then track the retention and work satisfaction scores for these two highly valued leadership groups. Going one step further, you could identify the top 20 percent of your organizational positions, in terms of criticality, and give a special weighting factor to all voluntary terminations that occur within these key positions. A few minutes of thinking along these lines can help you distinguish between metrics that are moderately interesting and those that are totally relevant.

When I say that metrics must be valid I mean that they should, in fact, measure what they are supposed to measure. Multi-rater feedback instruments provide a great example. Such tools are especially useful, but there are times when the scoring profiles that are generated from these instruments may not be particularly valid. Consider the situation in which managers are free to choose their own raters. In this case, long-term managers who are well-liked by their team members at the cost of not pushing for performance accountability know how "play the system" to get high scores. In contrast, if newly installed managers have been brought in to drive unpopular changes and to ramp up performance, they are at a serious disadvantage in slanting these assessments in their favor. The point is that you need to subject your talent performance metrics to careful review to ensure that they measure the dimensions that they claim to measure.

There are times when the metrics that you select may not only be invalid, but when their use may actually drive leadership behavior in a totally different direction from what you are intending. When you find yourself faced with this situation you will need to revise your metrics to make them congruent with your long-term talent management goals. Two examples are provided in Figures 10-2 and 10-3. Note that in Figure 10-2 executives have, in the past, been evaluated on their ability to identify at least two successor candidates to their own positions.

This type of metric often encourages executives to "make the numbers" by lowering their performance standards for successor candidates. This problem may be exacerbated when executives limit their reviews of successor candidates to those direct reports who have demonstrated a certain degree of loyalty and dutiful service. To resolve this situation, we can revise our metrics to encourage executives to review across the organization. Accordingly, our new metric would force leaders to identify potential candidates from across the entire company, and to indicate those non-selected candidates who were identified from areas other than their own immediate functions or departments. This step ensures that executives review the broadest field of candidates before nominating successors.

In addition, to minimize the likelihood of having executives nominate mediocre performers, we could mandate that candidates pass a rigorous and uniform screening process. Finally, we could

Figure 10-2. Example of how to revise metrics to minimize or eliminate drawbacks for a succession planning process.

Talent Goal	Talent Strategy	Initial Talent Metrics	Potential Drawbacks with Metric	Revised and Improved Metrics
To provide for continuity in succession, and minimize the disruption that could be caused by key leadership positions remaining open for a prolonged period of time, by pre-identifying qualified successors for key positions.	Use of talent stream strategy to identify exceptional successor candidates for targeted positions at, or above, the level of vice president.	Executives are evaluated on their ability to identify at least two successor candidates for their own positions.	Being an entitlement culture, managers tend to limit their successor nominations to their direct reports, and to base their nominations on such factors as loyalty and seniority.	A system of checks-and-balances is created in which all senior executives meet to compare their individual ratings of leadership potential for each identified leader.
				Executives are evaluated on the quality of their successor candidates, rather than the number of candidates whom they identify.
			To avoid poor evaluations, managers try to "fill in the blanks" on successor charts, regardless of the quality of those successors.	Executives are also required to produce lists of potential non-selected candidates whom they've considered from across their company.
				All candidates must past a screening process, in which they are identified as being in the top 20 percent of their talent base, as rated through 360° reviews, intelligence tests, and PA ratings.

institute a final step in which senior executives are brought together to compare their individual ratings of each candidate's potential for advancement. Together, these actions would help to
ensure that executives are evaluated on the quality of their successor candidates, rather than on the number of candidates that they
recommend for nomination.

A similar example is shown in Figure 10-3 for a career development planning process. In this case, to encourage leadership development, the organization has mandated that all leaders complete
a written career development form. As with our succession example, the use of this metric may cause managers to place so much
emphasis on "completing the forms" that they actually invest less
time conducting meaningful development discussions with their direct reports. In addition, these reports may come to adopt a cynical
attitude toward the concept of development planning, based on the
cursory discussions that are undertaken by their managers. More
meaningful metrics might involve having employees evaluate their
managers' effectiveness in conducting career development discussions, and the use of exit interview data that shows the degree to
which the lack of development planning has played a role in the
loss of talented leaders.

In each of these examples, spending a little more time on the
selection and design of performance metrics can go a long way
toward supporting an organization's bench-building efforts.

Step 2: Develop an Efficient Measurement System

The second step you can take to create an effective talent management evaluation process is to design an efficient measurement system. This means, in part, developing a measurement process that
is efficient, easy to implement, clearly interpretable and inexpen-
sive. In other words, it should be a measurement system that, once
designed, is easy to sustain. To clarify what I mean, assume that
you want to evaluate the effectiveness of your high-potential selec-

Figure 10-3. Example of how to revise metrics to minimize or eliminate drawbacks for a career development process.

Talent Goal	Talent Strategy	Talent Metrics	Potential Drawbacks with Metric	Revised and Improved Metrics and Measures
To encourage leader development and retention, and to ensure that individual career goals are aligned with evolving organizational requirements.	Employ a make/foundation strategy in which all managers are encouraged to obtain detailed information on the career goals of their direct reports.	The percentage of written career development plans that are completed for all direct reports.	Managers become focused on "filling out the forms" rather than engaging in in-depth career development discussions with their direct reports.	Employees complete annual evaluations in which they evaluate whether their managers have initiated career development discussions, and rate the overall quality of those discussions. The CTO conducts exit interviews with all identified HIPO leaders who have voluntarily terminated to determine the degree to which a perceived lack of development was a factor in their decision to leave the company, and whether the employee participated in a career development discussion within the past twelve months.

tion process. To measure your success in this area, let's assume that one of the metrics that you are considering is tracking the percentage of identified high-potential managers (HIPOs) who are promoted to broader positions over a three-year period. In this case, if you happen to work in a very large, geographically distributed organization that lacks a centralized human resource information system (HRIS) database, you'd probably want to consider the feasibility of being able to sustain this tracking process over the next several years.

The related question you'd want to ask concerns the *scalability* of your planned measurement approach; that is, will it continue to work for you five years from now, given the projected growth rate for your organization and the anticipated changes to your organizational structure? I know of one CTO who found that many of the data collection processes that his organization was using needed to be revised once it acquired another company. He realized, in hindsight, that his company's HR database couldn't "talk" to the HR database that had been developed by the acquired company. Moreover, for two years following the acquisition, the acquired company resisted attempts to divest itself of its own database. As a result, the CTO lacked real-time information on important talent metrics, such as manager performance and retention.

Another related issue is how to establish a system of checks and balances in your talent measurement process, in order to ensure that your organization's talent decisions are not driven entirely by a single metric or data source.

One way to establish a system of checks and balances is to implement secondary sign-offs on performance appraisals by your HR leader and the second-level manager. You might find it useful to extend sign-offs for high-potential nominations all the way up to your senior executive team. Such a process ensures that managers carefully think through talent decisions before they pass them on for approval, and that leaders engage their managers in in-depth discussions on leadership performance standards and the criteria that managers employ for nominating leaders to high-potential programs or successor candidacy.

Another step you can take to ensure that your talent management metrics are fair and balanced is to make use of multiple metrics and measures. In following this guideline, high-potential candidates might be assessed through combined scores on assessment center simulations, intelligence tests, and multi-rater assessment instruments.

Finally, there is a variety of third-party research firms—such as the Center for Creative Leadership, the Corporate Leadership Council, and the Society for Human Resource Management (SHRM)—that perform periodic reviews of the comparative utility of different talent measurement systems. Consider using these resources to determine whether the metrics and measurement systems that you have selected are representative of those used by world-class organizations.

Step 3: Establish a Baseline for Comparison

So let's assume that you've carefully selected metrics that are relevant and valid, and measurement systems that are easy to use. The next question is how to interpret these metrics. If an executive takes a 360° multi-rater instrument and scores a 4.75 out of a possible score of 6.0 on the subscale of "strategic thinking," is this score indicative of a problem or of leadership strength? The only way that you can tell is to make use of a broad database that can provide a yardstick for comparison.

One of the most important advantages of some of the assessment instruments that are offered by large, international consulting firms is that they employ robust normative databases that contain comparative information from thousands of leaders across a variety of organizations, industries, and countries. Some of the leadership assessment instruments that I personally prefer are:

- The 360° Benchmark® instrument marketed by the Center for Creative Leadership

- The assessment center instruments offered by DDI (Development Dimensions International) and PDI (Personnel Decisions International)

- The e-Choices® learning agility instrument developed by Lominger, LLT

- The ASSESS personality instrument developed by Bigby Havis Consulting

- The employee engagement survey offered by the Corporate Leadership Council

Please note that I'm not formally endorsing the use of these instruments (that's a decision that you will need to make after careful review with your senior executive team). However, I have found that the use of such testing and survey instruments can provide a rich backdrop for helping you interpret the test scores of your own leaders.

Inter-organizational databases are particularly useful when you are working within an insular organization that has traditionally looked inward to assess the potential of its leaders and to identify replacements for key positions. Under these conditions an organization can delude itself into thinking that its leadership population constitutes a reasonable universe for comparison. This problem is compounded if the organization in question has failed to carefully track the performance of its competitors, or if it has developed an entitlement culture that has fostered low performance standards. For a better understanding of the important role that external benchmarking can play in helping you to strengthen your leadership bench, I invite you to reread the sidebar example provided in Chapter 7.

Step 4: Establish a Means of Reinforcing Key Performance Areas

The best performing companies make their managers and executives accountable for leadership development. This conclusion was recently borne out by a 2005 research study entitled *How the Top 20 Companies Grow Great Leaders*, which was jointly sponsored by Hewitt Associates and The Human Resource Planning Society (HRPS). This study attempted to identify the top twenty companies for growing talent, out of 370 U.S. companies that were evaluated by an independent panel of judges.[1] The study found that 80 percent of the top twenty companies held their managers and senior executives accountable for the success of such programs as succession planning and performance management. By comparison, only 35 percent of the 350 other companies reviewed in this study held their managers and executives accountable for talent management. Instead, they were much more likely to pass on responsibility for the success of talent management to their HR departments.

One way to encourage managerial accountability for talent management is to tie performance in this area to executive compensation. This statement is borne out by another finding from the Hewitt and HRPS "Top 20" study, which was that, compared with their lower performing counterparts, the top twenty companies identified in the study tended to focus a much higher percentage of executive compensation on their managers' ability to develop organizational leaders.[2]

In addition, consider making leadership development a key performance category in your annual performance appraisal process. Similarly, you may want to fold the following selection criteria into your nomination and assessment process for identifying high-potential managers:

- To what degree is this executive able to develop junior-level leaders?

- To what degree does this executive make himself or herself available to mentor and coach other managers?

- How would you rate this manager's ability to make good leadership talent calls on hiring and promotional decisions?

- What is the caliber of the candidates who are nominated by this leader for high-potential or succession programs?

- How effective is this leader in managing difficult talent decisions, such as making a determination on whether an individual is ready to take on a difficult development assignment, or determining when a performance improvement plan needs to be initiated for a manager?

Step 5: Get Stakeholders Aligned on How Metrics and Measures Will Be Employed

The final step that you can take to create an effective measurement system for your talent management efforts is to work to ensure that your senior management team agrees on how talent metrics and measures will be employed in your organization. When attempting to secure this alignment I generally follow the following eight steps:

1. Reconfirm with your senior team your long-term (three- to five-year) leadership talent goals, the intended outcomes of those goals, and your primary talent strategy.

2. Because the success of any business measurement process is to focus organizational attention on a few key metrics, provide your senior team with a breakdown of all organizational talent management activities, including executive recruiting, retention, development, high-potential selection, and succession planning.

Ask your senior team to help you rank these areas according to their relative impact on organizational performance.

3. As your first-year goal, work on instituting metrics for the top two areas that are identified through this ranking.

4. Prior to meeting with your team, prepare a split-sheet list outlining proposed metrics for each of the areas included in your ranking, and your assessment of the respective advantages and disadvantages associated with each of these metrics. Some of these factors might include the comparative ease of implementation for each metric, as well as their relative cost, utility, and validity. One final feature you should consider is the degree of difficulty involved in obtaining sufficiently accurate and detailed data on each metric.

5. Using this split-sheet list, work with your senior team to select no more than two metrics and associated measures for each of the two talent management activities that you've selected.

6. For each of these activities under review, agree on how you define "success." For example, with respect to executive retention, success might be defined as "decreasing the current loss rate for high-potential leaders in manager-director positions from a current level of 15 percent per year to 10 percent per year."

7. Reach agreement on the respective roles that your HR department, CTO, and line managers will be expected to play in gathering and tracking this information. Also reach agreement on how often your senior team will want to review this information, and the preferred vehicle for this review. (In other words, will a simple quarterly e-mail or memo suffice, or does the review of this information merit a slot on the senior team meeting agenda?)

8. Decide whether it makes more sense to spend a few months testing the use of the proposed metrics and measures with a single department or business division before launching them across your organization.

Notes

1. *Research Highlights: How the Top 20 Companies Grow Great Leaders*, Hewitt Associates, LLC., 2005.
2. *Ibid.*

CHAPTER 11

MAKING MID-COURSE
CORRECTIONS

No matter how far you have gone down the
wrong road, turn back.

—TURKISH PROVERB

No matter how carefully one constructs and implements an organizational talent strategy, occasionally every manager makes talent decisions that either prove to be wrong or that need to be reexamined based on evolving organizational requirements. The trick is to develop "early alert systems" that quickly signal that a talent decision isn't working, and then take actions to correct it. In this chapter I'll provide suggestions for managing two different types of mid-course corrections on talent management. The first involves making changes to ineffective talent strategies, while the second involves correcting ineffective talent deployment decisions.

When and How to Make Changes to Your Talent Strategy

Earlier, in Chapter 9, I stressed the importance of remaining flexible and adapting one's strategy to changing conditions. Quite often

219

we find that this requires not just a subtle refinement of tactics, but a complete review and subsequent overhaul of one's talent strategy. Inevitably, when this situation occurs it is because the underlying conditions that drove a talent strategy have dramatically changed. Accordingly, it's important to continually monitor those underlying conditions to see whether you are now operating under a different organizational and environmental scenario. Let's briefly consider how changes to leadership strategy play out in both a "critical-event" scenario and an "incremental-change" scenario.

The Critical-Event Scenario

At some point, your organization may encounter a catalytic event that clearly signals the need for a change in your leadership talent strategy. To illustrate this, consider the following hypothetical case:

A large consumer products company that's been operating exclusively in the U.S. market, has traditionally relied on internal development and targeted succession (the Make and Stream Strategies) to fill its leadership pipeline. While this has worked quite well in the past, things are about to change. The company purchases a smaller firm that's headquartered in Germany and distributes its own products throughout Central Europe. The acquiring company's CEO decides to cross-pollinate his leadership talent pool by identifying those future leaders who have the flexibility, learning agility, and sophistication to work comfortably within both of these different work cultures and environments. His challenge to his CTO is to consider whether the talent management strategy that his company has had in place for the past ten years is well aligned with these new challenges. *Faced with this situation, what would you recommend?*

Here is a one possible solution:

You determine that the problem with retaining the Stream Strategy is that too many leadership assessment, successor, and placement decisions will be made separately by each of your two organizations, without consideration as to the ability of successor and HIPO candidates to work across organizational boundaries. In addition, this approach may not provide your corporate office with full visibility to emerging leaders within the new acquisition. Finally, this approach does little to create a common learning environment, nor does it provide you with an opportunity to compare the respective capabilities of leaders across these two organizations.

Based on this assessment, you may decide that the most reasonable course of action is to launch an integrated, high-potential talent pool, comprised of three, interrelated talent pools. Two of these pools could be limited to junior-level (first-line and mid-level) managers, with each pool exclusively dedicated to one of the two business organizations. These two pools could then serve as feeder-points for a single, higher-level talent pool that would involve the most promising candidates from each of the respective junior pools. By working through an integrated development experience, the participants of this senior-level talent pool would learn to incorporate best practices from each location, and would build personal networks that would span the two organizations. Moreover, such an option would serve as a great "fishbowl" experience—a development experience that, through vehicles such as 360° reviews and business simulations, could allow senior executives to learn more about the comparative strengths and weaknesses of pool participants.

Your own solution to this hypothetical change scenario may have been somewhat different, but the learning point is that whatever your decision, it would have probably required the complete and rapid overhaul and revision of your existing talent strategy.

The Incremental-Change Scenario

Obviously, not all change scenarios are this abrupt or dramatic. In many cases, your organization may encounter a slow but steady change wave that causes you to reexamine the respective tradeoffs associated with your current leadership talent strategy. Four examples of such changes are presented in Figure 11-1.

In these scenarios, the challenge you face is preventing the change from gradually sneaking up on you. To prevent this from happening, you'll need to identify those change indicators that begin to flag the need for change. Three such indicators are:

1. A gradual thinning out in the size and quality of your talent pipeline (discovering that, for the past four years, the number of nominations submitted for your high-potential leadership program have been decreasing at an average rate of 10 percent per year)

2. Encountering situations in which your organization is left relatively unprepared to meet new organizational or environmental changes (realizing that, with a pick-up in the economy, it has become more difficult to retain your best leaders)

3. A downward trend-line on your key performance metrics (such as receiving a steady decrease in the assessed quality of new hires, as evaluated by ratings on their performance appraisals twelve months after hire)

Gaining Executive Alignment on Changes to Strategy

Regardless of which of these two change scenarios signal the need for a change in your own talent strategy, once you've determined that a shift in strategy is in order, you will need to work with your senior team to explore the feasibility of making a strategy shift. The following nine-point plan may prove helpful in managing these discussions:

1. Provide your senior team with a brief review of the leadership talent strategy that is currently in play and the business assumptions on which this strategy was initially based.

Figure 11-1. Factors that may cause you to reevaluate your talent strategy.

Your Current Talent Strategy	Changes that Are Impacting Your Strategy	Required Revisions to Your Strategy
Up to now you've relied on a make/foundation strategy to support the large-scale development of your overall leadership talent base.	But your organization is attempting to make inroads in a completely new market—one that will also require the rapid adoption of new technology.	Requiring you to jumpstart these efforts by switching to a talent buy/trade-up strategy, and importing key change agents into your company.
For the past few years your new company has employed a buy/build-out strategy to quickly exploit an exploding market.	But you now have in place the bulk of the leadership talent needed to drive your business. Your challenge now becomes building a sustainable talent base, and giving more attention to the issues of succession and retention.	So you will begin to deemphasize your external search efforts, to focus more on a make/stream strategy that targets successors for your most critical leadership positions.
So far you've been able to rely on informal networks to fill leadership positions with qualified managers.	But your customer base is becoming much more diverse—a factor which isn't reflected in your senior management structure.	As a result, you've decided to supplement your standard search approaches with nontraditional sourcing, such as outreach programs to professional associations for diverse groups of managers.
So far your company has relied on management nominations and performance appraisal data to select qualified HIPO leadership candidates. Each division is annually allocated a certain number of HIPO slots, and in previous years you've had no problem using this process to obtain a strong pool of candidates.	But you realize that your leadership pipeline has thinned out over the past few years, due to a high percentage of executives who have entered retirement. Looking ahead, the picture gets worse as more of your leaders become eligible for retirement over the next few years.	Consequently, you will need to look across your enterprise for the best candidates for your HIPO pool. From now on, HIPO selection will be competitive across your company, and additional selection measures, such as intelligence tests and 360° feedback, will be use to provide a system of checks-and-balances on candidates.

2. Summarize some of the business and environment changes that your organization is now facing that have forced you to reassess this strategy. Ask your senior team for their assessment of the perceived impact of these changes on your organization.

3. Provide your team with a brief written outline of the changes that you are proposing to your current leadership talent strategy and the respective trade-offs involved, e.g., what your organization is likely to gain or lose by making these changes.

4. Explain what changes to resources and talent infrastructure may be needed to implement the proposed strategy shift. This might include an explanation of whether additional staffing or funds may be needed, any support that you require from your senior team, and any changes to policies, procedures, and executive compensation programs. At the same time, provide your team with a proposed timeline for implementing these changes.

5. Secure your senior team's agreement that a change to your talent strategy is warranted at this time, and that they are committed to securing the resources and support needed to make this change.

6. Discuss next-step actions that you'll need to take over the next few months to begin to implement these changes. As an example, you may decide that your organization needs to make the transition from a strong Make/Foundation Strategy to one that will rely heavily on hiring best-in-industry talent. In this situation, one of your first-step actions may be to review your current relationships with executive recruiting firms to determine whether you need to revise the scope of work or contract agreements for these firms. At the same time, you may need to determine whether the firms that have served you in the past are adequate to support your future direction.

7. Review changes to accountabilities for major program activities. If your change in strategy will require the formation of your company's first leadership talent pool, who will direct this activity? If you are the CTO, how will your charter and leadership role change under the new strategy?

8. Review the metrics and measures on which the new strategy will be evaluated.

9. Finally, reach agreement with your team on what will need to be communicated to your executives and other organizational members about this change in strategy, and in what form these communications should take place.

Correcting Bad Moves

The second type of mid-course correction involves rectifying ineffective talent deployment decisions. It is important to acknowledge to yourself that being a good talent strategist doesn't mean that you're omniscient. In most large organizations, at any one time a CTO or senior executive might be asked to weigh in on dozens of decisions regarding executive assessment, hiring, placement, retention, and severance. Occasionally, some of these decisions will be based on faulty or incomplete information, leading to bad hiring and bad promotional decisions. One of the actions that you can take to control or minimize such problems is to learn to recognize the warning signs of a bad move, particularly those related to hiring or promotional decisions.

The Six Warning Signs of a Bad Hiring Decision

Let's start with hiring decisions. During the first six months that a new leader is on board with your organization, there are six warning signs can alert you to the fact that your new hire is headed for trouble:

1. *Delayed Judgment Calls.* The manager may appear hesitant to make decisions and take actions. Certainly all managers have to get their footing before they tackle a new job in a new company. However, watch for the manager who appears to be all talk and no action, or who appears caught in "analysis paralysis." If your newly hired manager appears stuck on a major decision, ask two reasonable questions:

- "What information do you feel that you have to have in hand before you can make this decision?"
- "What actions are you taking to get this information, and how long will it be before you are ready to take action?"

The manager's responses to these questions will tell you whether he is simply making an astute assessment of the situation, or is having trouble taking risks and being accountable for decisions.

2. *Bad Judgment Calls.* These may involve decisions that appear to reflect a lack of experience or technical knowledge. More often, they'll be decisions that betray a high level of ignorance about how you do things in your organization. For example, you may work in an organization in which important decisions are always routed through chain of command. A bad judgment call that reflects an ignorance of your culture would be a newly hired leader who makes a large, high-risk contractual commitment on behalf of your company with an outside supplier without first getting approval and authorization from his direct manager.

3. *A Reluctance to Relocate.* Occasionally you'll find yourself hiring a manager who continues to find reasons for not relocating to your organizational site. In my experience, if this behavior extends over a year, it may well indicate that the manager (or the manager's spouse or partner) is unwilling to make the final commitment to the move. If you have concerns regarding this issue, consider having an honest conversation with your manager, and

find out how the new job and location is measuring up to his expectations.

4. *Cultural Ignorance.* Every organizational culture has its own unwritten set of rules and norms. Watch for signals that your newly hired manager isn't picking up on these new cultural norms or may be having difficulty adapting to this new culture. Here you may find it helpful to borrow some of the suggestions for obtaining CTO alignment that can be found in Chapter 2.

5. *A Lack of Sponsorship.* A dangerous situation is when, after several months on board, the newly hired manager is unable to muster a strong degree of sponsorship for her actions. This problem shows up in a number of ways, including the inability to build a strong business case for new ideas, having difficulty getting on senior managers' schedules, and being unable to build a convincing business case to sell new projects. If you have concerns about this issue, ask the newly hired manager, "With whom, on our senior team, do you feel that you've built strong, influential relationships?" Later on, ask these executives to provide their feedback on the manager.

6. *Managers Who Generate "Heavy Wakes" in Their Paths.* Strong leaders are sometimes brought into organizations to take on the roles of change agents and innovators. As a result, you can always expect some degree of complaining whenever a strong leader is attempting to move people toward a totally new direction. Therefore, if you begin to hear complaints about the new manager's leadership style, take the time to determine whether these complaints are simply background noise emanating from people who are change-resistant or are reflective of deficiencies in the manager's leadership style.

The Five Warning Signs of a Bad Promotional Decision

Now let's consider the case of those leaders who are promoted into larger roles with disastrous effects. Quite often, such problems are not due to a lack of technical competence or relevant background experience, but rather to interpersonal and communication issues that begin to surface as soon as the manager or executive is thrust into a new, more demanding set of business challenges.

A great deal of research has been done on how such leadership behaviors as insensitivity to others, the failure to build relationships with team members, peers, and senior managers, and unbridled arrogance can cause previously successful managers to crash and burn at some point in their careers.[1] These derailers tend to be part of the "signature features," or defining characteristics, of a derailing manager's leadership style. Available research suggests that in many cases, the underlying problem is that the leader who is facing derailment may be somewhat blind to the impact of his leadership style.[2] A related problem is that many managers who face derailment may be either unwilling or unable to make changes to their leadership style to meet new and different work conditions.[3,4]

As with bad hiring decisions, it's a lot easier to address derailment issues when we catch them early in the process. With that said, here are five warning signs that may signal that a promoted manager is headed for trouble:

1. *Being "Lost in Scope."* Watch for signs that newly promoted managers may not be able to scope up to the increased complexity and responsibilities of their new jobs. Some managers make use of a "close-quarter" management style that works with a small team, but translates into ineffective micro-management when the leader is promoted into a larger team comprised of more experienced professionals. This problem can also arise when a leader is promoted from a management role that involves the management of day-to-day transactional activities, to assume a higher-level role that requires the ability to think strategically, to deal with a higher level of ambiguity and complexity in their new jobs, and to manage entirely through other managers.

There are certain behavioral signs that a manager may be lost in scope. The manager's team members may complain that the leader appears to be reluctant to let go of responsibilities or to delegate assignments. Peers may note a lack of contributions from the leader during discussions of key projects or job issues, and the leader's manager may find that the leader is blind to emerging threats or opportunities because he lacks the ability to see and correctly interpret broader changes in the business and organizational environment.

2. *Excessive Stress.* The leader who is overwhelmed by new responsibilities or who is having difficulty making adjustments to new work conditions may become increasingly anxious or stressed. However, since newly promoted leaders are hesitant to look bad in the eyes of their bosses, don't expect recently promoted leaders to disclose any anxiety or hesitation that they might have about their new jobs. Instead, this anxiety will frequently reveal itself indirectly, in that the leader may appear far more short-tempered, emotionally volatile, and tense.

3. *Employee Complaints.* Look for complaints from the new manager's work team, peers, and internal customers that the new manager is difficult to work with, adversarial, and unable to adapt or change. More importantly, watch the newly promoted manager's reactions to these criticisms. A high level of angry defensiveness, an unwillingness to listen to feedback, and the tendency to respond to this type of critical feedback with attacks on the speakers, are all sure signs that the manager may be having serious difficulty.

4. *Excessively Insular.* Each time managers are promoted or transferred into new job functions, they face the task of building a new base of influence and support. Begin to worry when the newly promoted manager cuts herself off from others, hides in her office, and shows signs of being increasingly territorial. Check with the manager's peers to see whether she is reaching out to those around her.

5. *A Lack of Sponsorship.* As with the newly hired leader, another sure signal of promotional difficulties is when the newly promoted manager doesn't appear to have a strong base of support outside of his immediate manager. If, after several months in the new job, other senior managers indicate that they "don't have a clear read" on the newly promoted leader, or have difficulties with some of his decisions and actions, you will certainly need to probe further.

How to Confirm the Existence of Potential Leadership Problems

When you encounter a potential problem situation with a newly hired or recently promoted manager, you'll want to check your facts. In doing so, here are a few guidelines that might prove helpful:

• First, present your concerns to the manager and get his response. As a general rule, I find that the best performers are more open to feedback and don't easily become defensive in these types of discussions. A good sign is when the manager asks probing questions to try to find out more about the issue. A bad sign is when the manager goes immediately on the attack, rationalizing his behavior and attacking others who may be sharing their concerns.

• Go back to the source and find out whether the complaints are originating from your superstars, or from your poorest performers and chronic whiners.

• Look for managers on your team who can provide dispassionate and balanced feedback on the manager's leadership style, and ask for their read on the situation.

• As another step, conduct informal interviews with a few representative members of the manager's team to get their reactions.

• If the new manager has been with your company for several months, take a more involved step by asking your HR department to conduct a 360° review on the manager to obtain a more detailed view of her interpersonal and communication strengths and weaknesses.

- If you have the opportunity, look for an opportunity to see the manager in action, as he conducts a staff meeting, directs a project team, or confers with a peer or direct report. Observe not only the manager's behavior, but others' reactions to this leader.

- A final option is to go back and track down information that can help you determine whether the leadership behavior that you are encountering is indicative of a long-term performance issue. For a newly hired manager, consider going back to the references that were originally provided during his hiring process. For a recently promoted leader, you may wish to talk with her previous manager, or those HR managers who have previously worked with her. In either case, share your concerns and ask for their feedback, explaining that you are attempting to honestly assess the situation. Then determine whether the manager you are working with needs additional guidance and coaching.

Taking Action

Let's assume that you do indeed discover that you have encountered a serious problem with a newly hired or promoted manager. Obviously you can't turn back the clock and reverse the decision. What's left are five alternatives, presented in order below, from the simplest and most innocuous to the most extensive. A good starting point for action is to discuss the possible repercussions of each action with a trusted confidant, such as your senior HR leader or CTO. Take your time in considering your course of action, but once you've decided, act quickly and decisively:

1. *Talk to the problem manager and provide feedback.* It may simply be that the new manager doesn't understand how his leadership style is affecting others around him.

2. *Provide a brief on-boarding meeting.* The manager may accurately perceive her behavior but fail to know how it is interpreted by others within the new business context or corporate culture. This is the time to pull her aside and explain the kinds of behaviors and values that leaders are expected to display in your organization, and the types of leader performance that can lead to derailment in your company. A second option is to ask another senior-level manager, one who has the manager's trust and who is not in a direct reporting relationship, to initiate this conversation.

3. *Provide more extensive coaching.* If, after being given feedback on his behavior and information on the prevalent leadership norms in your organization, the leader is still encountering difficulties, you may want to provide him with coaching assistance from your CTO or from an external executive coach.

4. *Place the individual on a performance improvement plan.* If the problem you are encountering is seriously jeopardizing the leader's performance and appears to be more than a brief, transitory problem, you may need to meet with your HR executive or CTO to draft a written performance improvement plan. Such a plan should summarize the current performance, expected performance, the actions the leader is expected to take to get his performance back on track, and the timeline for improvement.

5. *Take action to demote, transfer, or remove the individual.* You'd hate to think that it might come to this but if it does, develop a solid plan for transitioning the new leader out of your organization. Once decided, act on this plan without delay or reservation. Once again, your HR leader or CTO can provide you with helpful guidance in managing this process.

Putting It All Together

In closing, it might be appropriate to provide a brief summary of some of the major themes that I've attempted to advance in this book. First and foremost, if there is one point that I'd like to leave you with, it's that the success of any talent management effort depends far less on the tools and tactics that a CTO chooses to employ than on the CTO's ability to develop and clearly communicate a viable talent strategy.

A second key theme is that the starting point for forming a talent strategy is to learn more about your company's business strategy, then explore how this evolving business strategy is likely to shape both your organizational structure and the roles and expectations you hold for your leaders. In other words, the savvy CTO "takes the point position" for his organization by attempting to anticipate the leadership skills and experiences that his organization will require over the next few years, and then assess the degree to which these needs are addressed through the organization's current bench strength.

A third major theme is that a good talent strategist is able to avoid getting lost in talent decisions. As I've attempted to show in Chapters 4 to 7, there are five key decisions that play a pivotal role in shaping leadership talent strategies. CTOs can add tremendous value to their organizations by helping their executive teams evaluate the relative trade-offs that are associated with each of these decision options.

Finally, in Chapters 8 to 11, I have attempted to make the point that a good strategy has to proceed smoothly from planning to flawless execution. This is reflected in a CTO's ability to identify valid performance metrics for evaluating the success of the organization's talent management efforts. It also requires the ability to use war-game scenarios to test the viability of one's talent management plans, the ability to deploy leadership talent in a way that effectively leverages the full strength of one's management team, and the ability to recognize problems when they surface and to make needed mid-course corrections.

While these themes are not meant to serve as a panacea for all talent issues, I believe that when taken together, they point to some of the key steps that we, as HR leaders and line managers, can take to increase the depth and versatility of our leadership teams.

Notes

1. Michael M. Lombardo and Robert W. Eichinger, *Preventing Derailment: What to Do Before It's Too Late.* Center for Creative Leadership (Greensboro, N.C.: CCL Press, 1989).

2. Jean Brittain Leslie and Ellen Van Velsor, *A Look at Derailment Today: North America and Europe.* Center for Creative Leadership (Greensboro, N.C.: CCL Press, 1996).

3. Michael Lombardo, Marian Ruderman, and Cynthia Mc-Cauley, "Explanations of Success and Derailment in Upper-Level Management," *Journal of Business and Psychology* 2, 3 (1988): 199-216.

4. Morgan McCall and Michael Lombardo, "Off the Track: How and Why Successful Executives Get Derailed," *Technical Report No. 21* (Greensboro, N.C.: Center for Creative Leadership, 1983).

Index

235